Practical Web Development

Learn CSS, JavaScript, PHP, and more with this
vital guide to modern web development

Paul Wellens

BIRMINGHAM - MUMBAI

Practical Web Development

First published: July 2015

Production reference: 1240715

Published by Packt Publishing Ltd.
Livery Place
35 Livery Street
Birmingham B3 2PB, UK.

ISBN 978-1-78217-591-9

www.packtpub.com

Credits

Author
Paul Wellens

Reviewers
Jorge Albaladejo
Elvis Boansi
Adam Maus
Jesús Pérez Paz

Commissioning Editor
Edward Gordon

Acquisition Editors
James Jones
Sonali Vernekar

Content Development Editor
Ritika Singh

Technical Editor
Ryan Kochery

Copy Editors
Alpha Singh
Ameesha Green
Jasmine Nadar

Project Coordinator
Milton Dsouza

Proofreader
Safis Editing

Indexer
Rekha Nair

Production Coordinator
Manu Joseph

Cover Work
Manu Joseph

About the Author

Paul Wellens has been a senior product manager for a major computer company in the Los Angeles area and Silicon Valley for over two decades. Before that, he used to install Unix systems and train companies in Europe, from his native Belgium. Later in his career, he became a web development aficionado because it brought him back to another passion of his: programming.

This is not his first book. His prior publication is of a different nature. Nature is what it is all about as it is a guidebook on Eastern California, which is illustrated with his own photographs. Therefore, it should not come as a surprise to learn that, besides experimenting with new web technologies, his major hobbies are photography and hiking in the Eastern Sierra.

Acknowledgments

I have written books before and I know that the result can only be successful if there are some nice people to assist you. This is the first time that I have worked with a publisher, Packt Publishing, so these are the first people I would like to thank. I would like to thank Shivani Wala for discovering me and James Jones for working with me to figure out the right book for me to write and for you to read. I enjoyed working with Priyanka Shah, Ritika Singh, and Ryan Kochery who assisted me in bringing this cool project to completion, without a single complaint, even though I was once again late with a deliverable. Thank you for being so patient with me.

I would also like to thank (yes, this is a note of cynicism) the three companies that "manage" the railroads in Belgium. Without their comedy of errors with trains — delays, cancellations, failure to depart because of mechanical problems, or trains departing from the station where you want to get to, as opposed to depart from, I would never had so much time to work on this book on my iPad. It is not in their honor, but, because for 2 years, it was the highlight of my day to safely arrive at Antwerp Central Station — which was rated by an American newspaper as the most beautiful train station in the world — that we decided to use it as the cover photo.

Next, I would like to thank my web developer buddy, Björn Beheydt, for taking the time to read the early versions of the chapters of this book and providing constructive feedback. I would also like to mention Steve Drach and Bart Reunes for always being there when I needed some technical advice.

Then, there are places that I would like to call a home away from home, where folks did not mind that I was typing away on my Bluetooth keyboard when inspiration kicked in. Most notably, I have to thank the folks at Trapke Op (Caro, Maressa, Evi, Klaartje and Jill) in Brecht, Belgium, where I typed these sentences. These wonderful people helped me make it to the finish line. Het Boshuisje in Zoersel, where Hendrik Conscience wrote books over a hundred years before I did, also comes to mind. I would like to thank Theo for always giving me a seat to land with my iPad, keyboard, and work.

Less related to this book, but still in need of a mention, are all my friends in California that inspired me to carry on doing great things in hard times. In particular, I want to express my appreciation to the people that work(ed) at the Gordon Biersch Restaurant in Palo Alto, which I can still proudly call my photo gallery. I thank them for their support for over 11 years and for still welcoming me when I visit them; they make me feel as if I only left last night. That also includes the patrons of the place with whom I've had numerous conversations and enjoyed every single one of them.

If you read this book, or my previous book, you will notice that I have a certain affinity and passion for a particular part of California. So, I would like to thank all the wonderful folks that live in the town of June Lake, California, for always having inspired me to come back and be creative. My goal in life is to go there as often as I can.

Finally, I would like to thank my mother. It has been hard for her since my father passed away and her son returned. I am dedicating this book to her, not that I expect her to read it, but I really appreciate the patience she had with me while I was writing it.

About the Reviewers

Jorge Albaladejo is a software engineer with a master's degree in information and communication technologies from HES-SO, Switzerland. With over a decade of experience building cloud, SaaS, and web applications, he considers himself to be a passionate and versatile full-stack web developer.

Throughout his professional experience, he has worked with many companies in different fields, such as project management, social networks, quality assurance, weather data visualization, and video games. He devours countless books about software engineering, project management, and science fiction, and he is passionate about clean, long-lasting software architectures.

He is currently working as a freelance contractor under the commercial name of CometaStudio, and he is mostly interested in start-ups and mid-sized companies that build great web experiences for great causes that make a difference. His next dream is to become a digital nomad who travels around the globe while working at the same time — and learn languages in the process!

Elvis Boansi is a software developer at John Jay College. He develops and maintains custom web applications that are used by members of the college. In his spare time, he enjoys playing soccer and basketball with his friends.

I'd like to thank my employers at John Jay College for all of their support. I would also like to thank my supervisors, Ana and Juan, for their feedback. I thank my friends, Sanga, Steve, and Loric, for constantly sharing their knowledge with me.

Adam Maus is a software developer with a master's degree in computer science and works at the Center for Health Enhancement Systems Studies at the University of Wisconsin in Madison in the United States. His interests lie in developing web technologies that utilize data mining to create better user experiences. He primarily works on websites that help people undergoing addiction recovery support, as well as people who are aging. In his free time, he enjoys running, biking, and reading books.

Jesús Pérez Paz is a full-stack web developer with experience in project management. He works at PepitaStore Inc. and collaborates with Mozilla.

His main area of work is design, and he integrates the user interface (or frontend) of web pages / applications; however, lately, he has been diving into backend stuff and has become a full-stack web developer.

He loves the open/free Internet and thinks that the Internet is a global public resource that must remain open and accessible to everyone.

www.PacktPub.com

Support files, eBooks, discount offers, and more

For support files and downloads related to your book, please visit www.PacktPub.com.

Did you know that Packt offers eBook versions of every book published, with PDF and ePub files available? You can upgrade to the eBook version at www.PacktPub.com and as a print book customer, you are entitled to a discount on the eBook copy. Get in touch with us at service@packtpub.com for more details.

At www.PacktPub.com, you can also read a collection of free technical articles, sign up for a range of free newsletters and receive exclusive discounts and offers on Packt books and eBooks.

https://www2.packtpub.com/books/subscription/packtlib

Do you need instant solutions to your IT questions? PacktLib is Packt's online digital book library. Here, you can search, access, and read Packt's entire library of books.

Why subscribe?

- Fully searchable across every book published by Packt
- Copy and paste, print, and bookmark content
- On demand and accessible via a web browser

Free access for Packt account holders

If you have an account with Packt at www.PacktPub.com, you can use this to access PacktLib today and view 9 entirely free books. Simply use your login credentials for immediate access.

Table of Contents

Preface

I am fortunate to have lived and worked in California for a long time. The majority of that time, I lived in Palo Alto, which is the center of Silicon Valley, the home of Stanford University, and the birthplace of many companies, big and small, such as Sun Microsystems, where I worked. I sat on the front row to see how the World Wide Web developed, as well as being present for the advent of social media. Facebook started on the other side of the wall of my favorite restaurant. Now, some Facebook guy or girl is sitting in what used to be my office at the bottom of the Dumbarton Bridge. As a product manager for Solaris, one of my tasks was to make sure that Netscape Navigator was included with our operating system. So, I was right at the source in which the development of the Web began. I even went to the Web 2.0 conference and bought the book of the same name.

Then, I felt the need to have my own website to display my photographs and inform people about the beauty and interesting places of the parts of California that I had discovered during my many journeys travelling around the state. So, I created one. One day, I was telling a friend about it and he tried to look at it on his mobile phone. It looked terrible. So, I bought a Nokia phone (a brick compared to what we have today) so that I could test my own site to make sure that it looked good on a phone as well. This is how I caught the bug of responsive design, years before someone started calling it this.

Upon my return to Belgium, I decided that it was time to learn as much as possible (I love to learn new things) about what is out there beyond creating websites and took a 6-month course on PHP web development. A lot of it looked familiar as I was previously a UNIX and C developer. There were only 12 people in the class, who were all bright minds, and I quickly discovered that there was more to learn.

As the classes took place in Leuven, a major university town in Belgium, I went to the local university bookstore and bought book after book on all kinds of related topics and quickly became a jQuery fan. jQuery, by the way, was not even included in the course. I started wondering why someone needed to have 35 different books to learn about web development and that writing a single book that gave a comprehensive overview of what you need to know to engage in web development would not be a bad idea.

Since then, web development has changed a lot; more books were needed, eBooks this time, but the concept remained the same. So, now you know why I wrote the book.

This book gives you an overview of all the general aspects of web development, in a traditional way, using plain HTML to do static websites, as well as the current way, to enable you to create your web pages dynamically and make sure that they look great on mobile devices as well, by using responsive design. We conclude by giving you a hint of what is yet to come if you replace the traditional web server by writing your own using node.js.

What this book covers

Chapter 1, The World Wide Web, gives you an overview of the history of what we know today as the World Wide Web.

Chapter 2, HTML, introduces HTML and gives you an overview of the most commonly used HTML tags to do web development. You will be able to create a basic website after reading this chapter.

Chapter 3, CSS, explains how to use Cascading Style Sheets (CSS). This is used for the presentation part or layout of your website, from color to dimensions to typefaces. The most commonly used CSS properties are explained here. Once you are done with this chapter, you will be able to make your basic website look good.

Chapter 4, JavaScript, first gives you an introduction to the world of programming and programming languages. Next, the overall syntax of JavaScript and how to use it for client-side programming is introduced.

Chapter 5, PHP, explains PHP, which is another programming language. This one is used to do server-side programming. It requires a web server to do the development of your website and deploy it. You will learn how to dynamically create your web pages, rather than having to write a bunch of HTML files.

Chapter 6, PHP and MySQL, introduces MySQL, an open source database. You will learn how to create a database, manage it using the phpMyAdmin tool, and perform basic CRUD (create, replace, update, delete) operations from within a PHP program.

Chapter 7, jQuery, covers a popular JavaScript library. It allows you to write more compact and clean code and handles browser incompatibilities for you. With this, it is going to be a lot easier and faster for you to write JavaScript code that traverses and manipulates the web page. It does so by using selectors, which you learned to use with CSS. So, with jQuery, you can write JavaScript code without having to learn a lot of JavaScript.

Chapter 8, Ajax, introduces Ajax. It represents a collection of techniques to make it easy to dynamically change only portions of a website. With this chapter, we have entered the world of what I call "modern web development". The interface that we use for our Ajax calls is jQuery.

Chapter 9, The History API – Not Forgetting Where We Are, explains a very important piece of the web development puzzle. Once we are changing pages on the fly so they look different but actually remain the same page (URL), strange things can happen when visitors want to go back to what they think is the previous page. A solution for this is described here that will not only work for HTML5 but for HTML4 as well.

Chapter 10, XML and JSON, describes XML and JSON. They are two popular formats to exchange data, for example the server and the client. Although XML is used in a variety of environments, JSON is closer to the web development community.

Chapter 11, MongoDB, describes an alternative to MySQL as a database. This is a so-called NoSQL database and a document database. Documents are conveniently in the JSON format. Here, how to access a MongoDB database from within a PHP program is described.

Chapter 12, Mobile First, Responsive Design with Progressive Enhancement, has the longest chapter title of the book. It explains how modern web development has to be done now that more people are using mobile devices instead of traditional computer screens to go to websites.

Chapter 13, Foundation – A Responsive CSS/JavaScript Framework, describes most of the features of the Foundation framework, which helps you with your responsive design. It contains everything that I have always wanted to write myself but never had the time to do. This concludes the part of the book that covers what I call modern web development.

Chapter 14, Node.js, gives an overview of what I call the avant-garde of web development. It introduces node.js, which allows you to write your server-side code in JavaScript, including your own web server, which is facilitated by using the Express framework.

Appendix, Bootstrap – An Alternative to Foundation, describes the popular CSS/JavaScript framework, which is an alternative to Foundation to help you with responsive design. The main reason to include this is to point out key differences and similarities.

The online chapter, *The Mono County Site*, provides a full example of a website or application where we apply most, if not all, the things we learned. It is available at `https://www.packtpub.com/sites/default/files/downloads/B03816_Appendix.pdf`.

What you need for this book

You will need the following software to work with the examples in this book:

Software	Source
Firefox and Firebug	`http://www.mozilla.org`
Apache Web Server	Part of the OS
XAMPP (includes MySQL and PHPMyAdmin)	`http://www.apachefriends.org`
MySQL	`http://www.mysql.com`
PHPMyAdmin	`phpmyadmin.net`
jQuery	`http://www.jquery.com`
The History jQuery plugin	`https://github.com/browserstate/history.js`
MongoDB	`mongodb.org`
Foundation	`foundation.zurb.com`
Node.js	`nodejs.org`
Bootstrap	`getbootstrap.com`

Who this book is for

This book is for anyone who wants to get to grips with the broader picture of web development today. It is perfect for beginners who want to get started and learn web development basics, such as HTML, but it also offers experienced developers a web development road map that will help them to extend their capabilities and gain a greater insight into how different technologies interact and work together.

Conventions

In this book, you will find a number of text styles that distinguish between different kinds of information. Here are some examples of these styles and an explanation of their meaning.

Code words in text, database table names, folder names, filenames, file extensions, pathnames, dummy URLs, user input, and Twitter handles are shown as follows: "We can include other contexts through the use of the `include` directive."

A block of code is set as follows:

```
<body>
<div id="header"></div>
<div id="container">
<div id="left"></div><div id="middle"></div><div id="right"></div>
</div>
<div id="footer"></div>
</body>
```

When we wish to draw your attention to a particular part of a code block, the relevant lines or items are set in bold:

```
<tag class="value1 value2">text<?tag>
```

Any command-line input or output is written as follows:

```
{ "key" : { "name":"Schwarzenegger","first":"Arnold",
"profession":"governator" } }
```

New terms and **important words** are shown in bold. Words that you see on the screen, for example, in menus or dialog boxes, appear in the text like this: " Now, not until a user clicks the **Beach** button, **Hello, World** will turn into **Hello, Beach**."

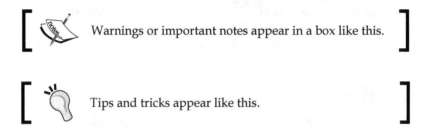

[Warnings or important notes appear in a box like this.]

[Tips and tricks appear like this.]

Reader feedback

Feedback from our readers is always welcome. Let us know what you think about this book — what you liked or disliked. Reader feedback is important for us as it helps us develop titles that you will really get the most out of.

To send us general feedback, simply e-mail feedback@packtpub.com, and mention the book's title in the subject of your message.

If there is a topic that you have expertise in and you are interested in either writing or contributing to a book, see our author guide at www.packtpub.com/authors.

Customer support

Now that you are the proud owner of a Packt book, we have a number of things to help you to get the most from your purchase.

Downloading the example code

You can download the example code files from your account at http://www.packtpub.com for all the Packt Publishing books you have purchased. If you purchased this book elsewhere, you can visit http://www.packtpub.com/support and register to have the files e-mailed directly to you.

Errata

Although we have taken every care to ensure the accuracy of our content, mistakes do happen. If you find a mistake in one of our books—maybe a mistake in the text or the code—we would be grateful if you could report this to us. By doing so, you can save other readers from frustration and help us improve subsequent versions of this book. If you find any errata, please report them by visiting http://www.packtpub.com/submit-errata, selecting your book, clicking on the **Errata Submission Form** link, and entering the details of your errata. Once your errata are verified, your submission will be accepted and the errata will be uploaded to our website or added to any list of existing errata under the Errata section of that title.

To view the previously submitted errata, go to https://www.packtpub.com/books/content/support and enter the name of the book in the search field. The required information will appear under the **Errata** section.

Piracy

Piracy of copyrighted material on the Internet is an ongoing problem across all media. At Packt, we take the protection of our copyright and licenses very seriously. If you come across any illegal copies of our works in any form on the Internet, please provide us with the location address or website name immediately so that we can pursue a remedy.

Please contact us at copyright@packtpub.com with a link to the suspected pirated material.

We appreciate your help in protecting our authors and our ability to bring you valuable content.

Questions

If you have a problem with any aspect of this book, you can contact us at questions@packtpub.com, and we will do our best to address the problem.

1
The World Wide Web

This book talks about the past, present, and future of Web Development. Beginning with *Chapter 2*, *HTML*, we will walk you through all the technologies you need to know about, in order to practice web development. Before we do that, we want to set the stage, so that we all know which Web we are talking about: this would be the **World Wide Web (www)**.

World Wide Web

I love history! So let us start with a little history about the World Wide Web. I was fortunate enough to be able to work at a company that developed the first commercial version of the UNIX Operating System. They were founded in 1977 and I joined them ten years later. UNIX is an Operating System (the thing you need to make your computer do something) that was intended to run on minicomputers (although they were called that, they could not fit into your apartment and required air-cooling). These computers were typically used as an isolated system that had quite a number of text-based terminals attached to them.

Today UNIX lives on, and forms the basis of Linux, Solaris, MacOS, and others. Our company spotted an opportunity to add products that would add features and technologies that today are standard. Some of these examples are email (ability to send a mail to a person on another computer), and ftp (ability to transfer a file to another computer, or to just access another computer). Yes, you had to pay extra if you wanted to be able to send mail. Thanks to the Internet, all of this was made possible.

The Internet

The Internet is a global network that today interconnects billions of computers worldwide. Its origin dates back to research done for the US government, but today everybody can get on the Internet, using its standard set of protocols, commonly referred to as TCP/IP (the IP here being Internet Protocol).

Every computer or device that is connected to the Internet will have a unique Internet address, aka IP address. It is a set of 4 numbers separated by dots, for example, 192.25.13.90. Of course, you will never tell your friend that you bought something at 192.25.13.90 but at, for instance, www.amazon.com. This is because the Internet also uses a feature that translates IP addresses into easier to remember domain names. The example I used happens to be a website you can go to and buy things from a practice that we all know has caused the www to become what it is today.

The Internet and the www are, in everyday speech, treated as if they are synonyms but they are indeed not. There are a lot of different services provided on the Internet (by companies called **Internet Service Providers (ISP)**), and that was already the case before the www existed (for example, giving you access to electronic mail). What it took for the www to emerge was (just like in JavaScript) a series of asynchronous events. Two of those are too important to not mention.

HTTP and HTML

You have probably heard this story many times, but the World Wide Web would not have existed without it. It is the story of Tim Berners Lee, an engineer at the **European Centre for Nuclear Research (CERN)**. The centre had many computers that were, of course, hooked up to the Internet. It also produced a tremendous amount of data and documents, and that became almost impossible to manage. Tim worked out a solution by developing a language to write these documents in, a protocol on top of the Internet to manage them, as well as a computer program for users to access them.

HTML

HTML, short for Hypertext Markup Language is the name of that language. Hypertext is text that contains **hyperlinks**, which in turn are those parts of a document which readers can click on to take them to a different document, using the link. You have all seen the blue underlined parts of a text, in not-so-good-looking web pages. These are hyperlinks.

A document in HTML consists of tags, with text in between them. There are opening and closing tags for example, as follows:

```
<h1>Hello, world</h1>
```

Here, `<h1>` is the opening tag and `</h1>` the closing one. We will learn about a similar markup language: XML. HTML and XML are not the same though. One important difference is that in XML you can define your own tags, as long as you close each one you've opened. XML is used to transfer the data and the tags are used to organize the data.

In HTML, tags do have a specific meaning. `<h1>` would be used in a document for the text of a level one header. A `<a>` tag—the anchor tag—is the one used to include the hyperlinks we just discussed. So the purpose of writing HTML is not to transfer data, but to present it to human users.

To do so, these tags are interpreted by the computer program we mentioned earlier. Such a program is called a **browser**. When the reader clicks on a hyperlink, the browser will detect that as well, and send a request to yet another program, the web server, to go fetch another document.

HTTP

This is where HTTP, the Hypertext Transfer Protocol fits in. If a user clicks on a link, it is like saying: go fetch another HTML document. The name of that document would be part of a longer string that starts with `http://` and also contains the domain name of the server. It is called a **uniform resource locator,** but we all refer to it as URL. Following is an example: `http://www.paulpwellens.com/examples/secondpage.html`.

What you can do with HTTP has evolved over time and we will learn about it later on in the book, but for now we need to move on with our history lesson. One more little tidbit of history for you: guess how our friend Tim called his browser, the first ever browser: WorldWideWeb. He later renamed it to avoid confusion.

The World Wide Web Consortium (W3C)

After he left the CERN in 1994, Tim Berners Lee founded the **World Wide Web Consortium (W3C)**. The consortium tries to enforce compatibility and agreement between vendors that deliver components for the web. Incompatible versions of HTML would cause browsers to render web pages differently; and incompatible features added to browsers have the same unexpected result.

If you visit www.w3.org, the consortiums website, you will notice that the W3C has evolved into a standards body for many technologies, but even in those days, having such an organization was sorely needed.

Mosaic

History moved on, and so did I! Our company was acquired by Sun Microsystems and I became product manager for our PC UNIX product. Oh yes, before I forget, PCs were everywhere by then and that phenomenon would, in the long run, also contribute to the explosion of the World Wide Web.

One day, in the year 1993, my engineering manager walked into my office, together with Jonathan, his lead programmer. They wanted to show me what he (Jonathan) had done over the weekend. It was a port (take the source code of a program and make it run as a binary on a computer) of a program called **Mosaic** for our PC UNIX product. I saw him type a few commands but did not quite understand why these guys were so excited. Little did I know that this seemingly innocent little program was going to change our lives forever!

The first browser

Mosaic was developed at the **National Center for Supercomputer Applications** (**NCSA**)at the University of Illinois in Champaign-Urbana (this is a long drive through cornfields from Chicago, which I took once) by a team led by Marc Andreesen. It was the first browser to support multiple protocols (hence the name) as well as display an image and text on the same page (surprisingly, this is not a trivial matter on a webpage!) It soon caught attention worldwide and the browser was ported to many platforms, so that more and more people could develop or have access to websites.

In November 1992, there were 26 websites. In the Mosaic browser, there was a *What's new* section that showed a new website everyday. Three years later, there were 10,000 and another three years later, millions. Today, I do not think it is possible to count them anymore. So how did we get from thousands to millions?

Netscape

Marc Andreesen founded a company, named it after Mosaic, and then later renamed it *Netscape Communications Corporation*. They basically rewrote the Mosaic browser and optimized it for environments with lower network bandwidth, such as individuals who access the Internet from home through their ISP. The browser was called **Netscape Navigator**. This was clearly the first commercial browser, making it to the shelves of computer retail stores as part of a bundle, Netscape Communicator.

Netscape was also credited as the first browser to include support for JavaScript. With this scripting language, interactivity could be added to web pages. The World Wide Web could be at anybody's fingertips, as long as you had Netscape. From 1994 to about 1999, Netscape clearly had the biggest market share for browsers.

Over time, Netscape was moved over to Mozilla Corporation, an Open Source organization, and the development of Netscape ended. Today, users can download the *Firefox* browser from `www.mozilla.org`.

Internet Explorer

Another derivative of Mosaic, Spyglass Mosaic, made it into the Microsoft codebase and was eventually bundled with Microsoft Windows. We know it today as *Internet Explorer*. This is how we reach the topic of the so-called browser wars. As I mentioned, Netscape was trying to win over as many customers as possible by getting into the retail market and charge for its browser. Microsoft, on the other hand, decided to bundle Internet Explorer *for free* in its Windows Operating System (of course you had to pay for Windows).

This led to many lawsuit-like situations as Microsoft was accused of unfair competition by the other browser vendors. This situation has now changed as all browsers are free. Computer users can today choose which browser they want to use. On tablets, choices are limited, but on the other hand, browsers on tablets usually have all the latest features.

A different and potentially more bloody war was going on at the technical level. Despite having a standards body, the W3C, which controlled and introduced new features (both HTML and CSS), not all browsers were adapting those features equally as fast. So the same web pages continued to look different when they were rendered by different browsers. Sad but true to say, the browser that was the most incompatible and unpredictable, Internet Explorer, was, by the turn of the century, also the one used by the majority of the people who would surf the web.

Developers therefore had no choice but to delay the use of new cool features at the expense of spending a considerable amount of extra time making their web pages look the same on a PC used by most visitors as it did on the system where they were created.

Things got far worse before they began to get better, as more developers started using JavaScript to add interaction and animation to the pages, whereas many System Administrators recommended a configuration with JavaScript switched off. Sometimes this resulted in the visitor seeing nothing at all on the page.

But do not despair, we are in 2015 now! In this book, we will take a different approach and always let you use the new features when the browser supports it.

The explosion of the Web

By the turn of the century, every company wanted to have a webpage. Web pages were created by linking more web pages, with information about the company or just the owner of the site. The latter was made possible by smart ISPs that also offered web hosting. People have to be able to access your site even while you or your computer is sleeping; so these services offer 24/7 uptime to put your HTML files. Web hosting companies also take care of getting you a domain name, such as www.thecoolestphotographer.com.

At some point, obtaining the domain name you wanted was bordering on another browser war, as there could only be one xyz.com, and if some entrepreneurial folks thought that having xyz.com first would be worth money, they would grab it.

When I wanted one for myself, paulwellens.com was already taken by a British rugby player, so I went for www.paulpwellens.com (P is my middle initial). I am neither British nor a rugby player so this was fine with me.

So a lot of pages were created worldwide, but all they had initially was information for you to look at, nothing else. In some cases, they were created once and never updated. That fortunately was the exception to confirm the rule. Many companies decided that they had to have a presence on the web and corporate websites were thus created. The advent of CSS facilitated this a lot, as it allowed the separation of presentation and content. That way, the marketing department would provide the corporate logo, and the look and feel, and all the other departments would provide the content.

Amazon.com and e-commerce

Some creative minds realized that the Web presented an opportunity to do more than just provide information. It is only a (relatively) small step from providing the information of the products you have on your site, to actually selling them. E-commerce was thus born. Amazon comes to mind as a good example of a site that everybody can relate to as being a **Web shop**. Developing a web shop of course involved a lot more than having someone in the company type in some content.

These products are real products; they sit in a warehouse, have a part number, a price, a name and description, different sizes and colors, and so on. That information, more than likely, is already present in some database that is updated each time a product is sold in a retail store. To sell something online, your webpage has to interact with the visitor, present him with some kind of an on-screen shopping cart, calculate subtotals, check warehouse inventory, and so on.

To do this, more and more programming was involved, and not just data entry into an HTML file anymore. So the job of Web Developer was born. Traditional programmers are skilled in a single programming language (Java or C++) and usually a single platform (**Solaris** or **.NET**). Web Developers have to be fluent in at least four different languages, as well as know a thing or two about databases. I would like to add one aspect which, to me, makes this job very exciting — one gets to be involved in design aspects. The gap between a Web Designer and a Web Developer is narrowing. So today, one talks about Front-End and Back-End developers.

So this is what we will teach you in this book; *how to be a Web Developer*, but not before wrapping up our history lesson. There are a few more things that made the web what it is today.

Google and Yahoo!

So you have a website with information, or a web shop because you are selling something on the web, like www.mycoolproduct.com. How do you expect to reach your potential customers, call every single one of them? This is where Google or Yahoo fit in. These popular companies developed the so-called search engines. You want to find out everything there is to know about a movie you just watched, a song you cannot remember the name of, or simply the phone number of your favorite restaurant? You visit google.com, yahoo.com, or equivalent sites and type in what you are looking for. Chances are you will find it.

We did a usability study at work where we gave one group a set of CDs, a stack of manuals, and a computer to install; the other group did not get the manuals but Internet access. The second group did way better because they felt they did not need the manuals, as they assumed them to probably be out of date, and immediately looked things up online. And this happened over 10 years ago.

Today, the use of search engines is so commonplace that terms like Yahoo! and Google are used as verbs. In some languages, they actually have become verbs and made it into the official dictionary.

Social networking

I know people who do not use Facebook today, but I do not know anybody who does not know of Facebook. For years I walked by the building where Facebook had its office. I was not really interested. Then, when I moved back to Belgium, I decided to join them so I could stay in touch with my friends in California, who live in a different time zone and several thousands of miles away. From one of them I found out that the Facebook folks have since moved into the building where I used to have my office. Funny how that goes sometimes!

Facebook, Twitter, YouTube, and LinkedIn are examples of popular social networking sites. Nothing is sold here, but shared. People share pictures, stories, events, thoughts, ideas, opinions, and so on.

Web development

Many years ago, I took a 6 month class on what, basically, is part one of this book. Months into it, it became apparent that the lack of an introductory part that explains how all the components of the course were related, was the course's biggest flaw.

After six months, there were still people who did not understand the difference between Java and JavaScript. So I promised myself two things: that one day I would write a book, and that such a chapter would be part of it. So let's go!

HTML

Files written in HTML form the basis of every website. We briefly touched on its history in the previous section; here we will dig a little deeper in its structure. Look at the following example:

```
<!DOCTYPE html>
<html lang="en">
<head>
  <meta charset="utf-8">
  <title>Hello World example<\title>
<\head>
<body>
  <h1>Hello, world<\h1>
<\body>
<\html>
```

The first line specifies DOCTYPE, referring to the HTML version used, so the browser knows how to interpret the file. The one in the example is indicative of HTML5. DOCTYPE statements used to be a lot longer.

This is followed by the main tag, the `<html>` tag. In-between, we will find all our HTML in two sections, `<head>` and `<body>`. The body tag is what contains your content, and the head tag contains other information. In our example, there is one metatag that specifies what encoding is used. The `<title>` tag contains text that will be displayed by the browser at the very top of the window. It is very important to not forget the `<title>` tag, as this is one of the things search engines will examine.

In this simple example, the body contains a single `<h1>` tag. This represents a level one header in the document, similar to headers you find in word processors. The browser will decide how to display that content or, as they say, render it. So how do we get the HTML into a file and how do we get it to a browser?

HTML editors and other tools

As an HTML file is just a text file, your favorite text editor will do just fine. Just make sure it has the `.html` extension in the name, for example `hello.html`.

However, at some point, you are probably going to include some CSS, JavaScript, and surely PHP in the same file, in which case specialized tools will make you far more productive.

Browsers and web servers

So now you have a file called `hello.html` and you want to look at it in a browser. In real life, this file will be part of your website and you will have to put it there. This is where the company that is hosting your website told you to put your files. They will give you all the information to correctly transfer your file(s) to their server.

They will end up in a folder that is called the **document root**, the root of all the files that make up your site. If you were to follow the instructions with the `hello.html` file and transfer it there, you will see the result when you type the following address in the URL bar of your browser:

```
http://www.mycoolsite.com/hello
```

You can also look at your file locally, and we will teach you more about that in the next chapter.

It is very important to realize that to the people who visit your site, your web page may not look the same as what you created. One factor — but not the only factor — is the browser that is being used. We therefor recommend that, from the early development stage on, you look at your work using different browsers and increase the number of browsers, for/and different devices.

Always install Mozilla Firefox and Google Chrome on your Mac or PC. Pick one to do your development (I like Firefox because of *Firebug*), but always do a little bit of testing with other browsers before you deliver.

So, start with our little example, and you will see that even *Hello World* will look different in different browsers. Fortunately, we can control almost all of this by using CSS.

CSS

Cascading Style Sheets (CSS) is a technology that works nicely in accordance with HTML and allows you, not the browser, to determine what your page will look like.

Look at this slightly modified example of our **Hello, World** webpage, `hello.html`:

```
<!DOCTYPE html>
<html lang="en">
<head>
  <meta charset="utf-8">
  <title>Hello World example</title>
  <link href="hello.css"   rel="stylesheet" ></link>
</head>
<body>
  <h1 class="green header" id="hello">Hello, World </h1>
</body>
</html>
```

In the line containing the `<h1>` tag, we added two HTML attributes, `class` and `id`, to the `<h1>` element. Attributes are strings inside an HTML opening tag of the format name="value" and the two most important attributes you can use are `class` and `id`. Many elements can be part of several classes, but `id`s are unique to a single element.

Now create a file called `hello.css` with the following content:

```
h1 {
  font-family:Baskerville, cambria, serif;
  font-size:24px;
}
.green {
  color:green;
}
#hello {
  font-weight:bold;
  font-style: italic;
)
```

This is our first CSS stylesheet. The first rule in the file means that any <h1> element in our document will be in the Baskerville font (or cambria, if Baskerville is not present on the user's computer), at 24 pixels, and in the color the browser has chosen (usually black).

However, when it, or any other element, not just h1, has a class="green" (in CSS, the . in name means class name), it will be displayed in the color green.

Finally, our specific **Hello World** header will be displayed in bold and italics because of the last few lines in the CSS file. The # character is used in CSS to indicate an identifier, so the **#hello** rule means a rule for the element that is set to the id= "hello".

As a result of all of this, any browser should render our HTML file as a line containing the text *Hello, world*, displayed in letter type Baskerville (a serif font often used for eBooks, no relation to Sherlock Holmes that I know of), in green, of size 24 pixels, and in bold and italic. Just try it, it works!

Note that we did not repeat the Baskerville line in the #hello rule, the rule is simply inherited. The <h1> rules cascade into #hello, as this happens to be an <h1>, hence the name Cascading Style Sheets. As we just demonstrated, we can clearly separate the content and the presentation of our page by using CSS. That is why it is important to learn how to use CSS as early as possible.

So, as a Web Developer, you already know that you need to master at least HTML and CSS. We will now move on to the next piece of the language puzzle—JavaScript.

JavaScript

When we talk about JavaScript in this book, unless noted otherwise, we mean client-side JavaScript. All the code is interpreted, just like the HTML and CSS, by the browser.

By using JavaScript, we can add action to our pages and interaction with the visitors of our website, as well as change the contents and look of our page through programming. Let us take a look at the following example:

```
<!DOCTYPE html>
<html lang="en">
<head>
  <meta charset="utf-8">
  <title>Hello World example</title>
  <link href="hello.css"   rel="stylesheet" ></link>
</head>
<body>
```

```
    <h1 class="green header" id="hello"></h1>
    <script type="text/javascript">

    var answer = confirm("Do you want to say hello?");
    if (answer == true)
    {

    document.getElementById("hello").innerHTML="Hello, world";
    }
    </script>
</body>
</html>
```

If you look at this page in a browser, there will be no **Hello, World** displayed on your screen, but a pop-up box will appear with a question. If you answer the question **Yes**, our familiar green **Hello World** text will be back. The pop-up box itself will look completely different when you use a different browser.

If you look at the code, you will recognize programming-like stuff. There is an `if` clause and there is a variable (answer). Note that the name of the variable is a normal character string but in its declaration it is preceded by `var`. All of the JavaScript code is in-between an HTML `<script>` tag with a `type` attribute of `text/javascript`.

There is one line that is very typical to JavaScript and does all the work for us:

```
document.getElementById("hello").innerHTML="Hello, world";
```

Chapter 4, JavaScript is where we will really teach you what this means. For now, we will give you the English interpretation of this line of code: In our document, replace the inner content of the HTML tag with `id` hello by the string **Hello, world**.

In subsequent chapters, we will introduce JavaScript `libraries`, which will allow you to write more compact JavaScript code, with a lot of work already done for you. **jQuery** is one of these libraries and will be discussed in *Chapter 7, jQuery*.

PHP

JavaScript is a complete language and allows you to do a lot more things than those we showed you in the previous little example. However, as I mentioned, this is client-side JavaScript, interpreted by the browser. So once you switch off your computer or tablet, it is all gone. Well, some of it may be saved on your machine.

Imagine trying to create an online store using only the languages we have mentioned so far. That would not work. The information of what is available in the store, as well as the data of your specific order has to live somewhere else. That would be the computer of the company that runs the store, not the device that runs the browser used to visit the site.

So, dear Web Developer, you have guessed it, you will have to learn at least one more programming language to deal with all of this, before you can create an online store. The language itself could be any of several (it can even be JavaScript), but where the code is stored and interpreted is the key difference here: a remote Application Server. One of the most popular of these languages is PHP, which is covered in detail in *Chapter 5, PHP*. Let us look at the following example:

```php
<?php
  $hello = "Hello World Example";
  $helloheader = '<h1 class="green" id="hello">Hello, World</
    h1>';
?>
<!DOCTYPE html>
<html lang="en">
<head>
  <meta charset="utf-8">
  <title><?php echo $hello; ?></title>
  <link href="hello.css"  type="text/css" rel="stylesheet"
></link>
</head>
<body>
<?php
  echo $helloheader;
?>
</body>
</html>
```

So far we have been able to test our little examples in a browser, but this is different. To try out this example, you will need to have an Application Server, local or not, installed. For now, just read on.

Notice the `<?php` and `?>` strings in the example. This is the beginning and end of where the PHP code resides and will have to be interpreted by that Application Server. The first portion of the code defines two variables. Note that in PHP, names of variables start with a $ sign, whereas in JavaScript they don't. `echo`, familiar to UNIX folks, simply echoes the value of these variables.

So once the AppServer is done interpreting the PHP code, all you are left with is our HTML example from the CSS section. This is exactly how it works: the AppServer interprets the PHP code, and then the WebServer passes the resulting HTML code to the browser.

Apache is the name of a very popular AppServer that happens to be a WebServer at the same time. This is software that runs on a computer we also call a server and this is where your program file resides: `hello.php`.

So `http://www.mycoolsite.com/hello` will be, once again, the way this webpage can be accessed. This may look like a little bit of using an overkill tour an additional language to display **Hello, World**. But there are some situations where you'd want to do so, for example if the data you need in your HTML is stored somewhere else.

Data

One of the main reasons to use the remote server and the server-side language is going to be the storage and manipulation of data. This data can be in several formats, from a flat text file to a spreadsheet, XML, JSON, or a full-fledged database, which requires a Database Server. In the latter case, you may need to learn yet another language, **Standard Query Language (SQL)** and deal with another (software) server: a database server. We will address several options in this book.

Summary

In this chapter we discussed the advent and history of the World Wide Web. Next we discussed Web Development in general with a few examples. In order to become a developer of Web Applications, you will have to master at least four languages: HTML, CSS, JavaScript, and a server-side language such as PHP.

Depending on how you plan to organize your data, there may be a need to learn a fifth language (SQL) as well. There will also be more things to learn, such as how to use a library or framework. The good news is that they all have their role in the overall picture of what a Web Application is all about.

Now that we know what we need to learn, let us go do it! We will start with HTML.

2
HTML

In this chapter, we will walk you through the basics of HTML. In *Chapter 1, The World Wide Web*, we already covered what the letters HTML mean, where the language comes from, and what it is used for: to create the content part of your web pages. We already know that this content is placed in between tags: `<tag>` to open and `</tag>` to close.

It would be beyond the scope of this book to provide a complete reference to all HTML tags, or elements (we will use these words interchangeably), and all of their attributes. There are some good references listed in the bibliography and of course there are some cool online references. I personally like `w3schools.com` but, if you don't, simply Google "HTML" followed by a tag name you would like to know more about and you will find some great alternate sources.

We will therefore only describe the most commonly used HTML tags in this chapter, grouped by the role they play in the document. For example, all the tags that can be used in a table are grouped under the heading `table`.

HTML versions

Since its creation, there have of course been several different versions and flavors of HTML. The most notable are HTML4, XHTML, and HTML5:

- **HTML4**: This is the last of a series of versions of HTML and is what most people will implicitly refer to when they talk about HTML.

- **XHTML**: This is a different definition of HTML and an attempt to make HTML a member of the XML family, giving it more strict rules. An advantage is that it would be easier to use tools and languages that are intended to manipulate and translate XML documents. However, interest in maintaining that standard seems to have faded.

- **HTML5**: This is the newest kid on the proverbial HTML block. A lot of books have been published about it and, if you have read one of them, you will have discovered that HTML5 is more than just a new version of the markup language. Granted, it comes with quite a few new tags, such as the `<nav>` or `<section>` tags. HTML5 also features the use of custom data attributes such as `data-whateveryouchoose` that you can use in your document. Later on you can manipulate these using JavaScript. It is a way to pass data along inside an element; hence the name chosen: `data-*`.

Did I say JavaScript? All the other new features in HTML5 are actually JavaScript APIs like HTML5 Canvas. Canvas lets you draw things on your web page, pie charts for example. Exciting as these APIs may be, they are beyond the scope of this chapter.

Semantic and presentational HTML

The approach we are taking in this chapter and in the first part of the book overall is to only use HTML elements and attributes that are covered by all three standards. In practice, this means we will not use any HTML4 attributes that disappeared in HTML5 and will not use any HTML5 elements or attributes that did not exist in HTML4.

On the other hand, we do not want to discourage the use of new things, so we will list HTML5-specific elements in a separate list. We will also use the new elements in the second section of the book where we introduce a cool CSS/JavaScript framework.

One could easily divide HTML elements into two groups. The first group consists of elements that refer to parts of a document: headers, paragraphs, tables, forms, lists, and so on. (`<h1>`, `<h2>`, `<p>`, `<table>`, `<ul>`). We call this semantic HTML as they refer to the names of things; they describe what they are.

Another group contains the elements used to indicate how things look: how they are aligned, which font is used, if it is in bold or italics, and so on (`<center>`, `<font>`, `<b>`, `<i>`), and we could call them presentational HTML. The same is true for HTML attributes. `class="green"` or `id="chapter"` would be semantic, while `width="150px"` or `valign="top"` would be presentational.

It is the recommendation of the W3C to use CSS for presentational things, and we follow that recommendation. This way will also avoid you learning a bunch of new things, only to later find out that they are no longer used, as most HTML4 elements and attributes that are no longer available in HTML5 happen to be presentational. The word you will find online to indicate that something is no longer used is *deprecated*.

When I first ran into this word I misread it as depreciated. That word might have been a better choice. Either way, if elements and attributes are labeled as such, avoid using them.

As a consequence, we are not going to show you pretty examples of HTML documents in this chapter, as the part that will make it pretty, CSS, will have to wait for a while until we get to *Chapter 3, CSS*.

The structure and syntax of an HTML document

An HTML document is a text file with a name ending in `.html`, for example, `hello.html`. A modern, minimal HTML document looks like this:

```
<!DOCTYPE html>
<html lang="en">
<head>
<meta charset="utf-8"/>
<title>Hello, world</title>
</head>
<body>
<h1>Hello, World</h1>
</body>
<html>
```

Doctype

The first line specifies the document type (`<!DOCTYPE html>`). Today, this can be as simple as the word `html` telling a browser that this file is to be interpreted as an HTML5 document. Documents written to the older specifications contain the name of that spec followed by a path to a **Document Type Definition (DTD)** file that can be used to examine the document for conformance. Things are a lot more flexible these days.

<html>

This is the root of the document. Everything in the remainder of the document will be inside this html tag. What is inside the html tag consists of two sections, the head and the body.

<head>

The head section contains one or more <meta> tags. The one in our earlier example specifies that the encoding of the text part of the document has to be in **UTF-8**.

This section is also where the <title> tag lives. The text inside this element is the text that will be displayed at the top of the browser window and is looked at heavily by search engines. So it is important to always include a title tag and for its contents to be correct and meaningful.

Furthermore, the <head> section is used to include more information that the browser will have to read before the body part of the document is loaded. Your most typical example will be the paths to the **CSS stylesheets** that are used for the document. We will have many examples in this book.

<body>

Inside the body tag is the core content of our document. As a consequence, if there are certain style elements that you want to be used in the entire document, you will be able to do that by simply styling the <body> tag. We will remind you about that later. Of course, we first have to learn what we can put inside the body.

Syntax for tags or elements inside the document

The syntax of an HTML tag is very simple:

```
<tag attribute1="value1" attribute2="value2">text</tag>,
```

This is followed by the next tag. You can place everything on a single line or every pair of tags on a separate line for readability as new lines and spaces in between tag pairs are ignored.

Inside the text portion, spaces are not ignored, but multiple spaces in a row are reduced to one. So if you want to insert more spaces, you will have to use a different method (See *HTML entities* later in this chapter).

For elements that have no content, there is a shorthand notation. We can use:

```
<tag/>
```

We use that instead of:

```
<tag></tag>
```

In our example, the shorthand notation is used for:

```
<meta charset="utf-8"/>
```

The `class` attribute can have multiple values, in which case it would be written like:

```
<tag class="value1 value2">text<?tag>
```

It is not written like this:

```
<tag class="value1" class="value2">text<tag>
```

This last line demonstrates a common oversight when a `class` attribute is added without realizing that a class attribute was already present. In this case, the second one will be ignored. The browser will also ignore all elements and attributes that are not recognized as HTML tags.

Unlike compilers for old school programming languages, you will never see an error message when you mistype something. Things will simply not look right or you may even get a blank screen. This is why it is extremely productive to use an HTML editor or other tool that recognizes tags and attributes as valid HTML ones, preferably tools that display them in color.

HTML comments

Anywhere inside HTML code, you can insert a comment: a reminder to yourself , for posterity, or (probably more important) for others in your team who need to share your code. The syntax is very simple. Anything that is inside an HTML block can be commented by putting `<!--` in the front of it and `-->` after it:

We recommend strongly inserting more comments rather than less. Applying comments is also useful when someone asks you to remove something from the website and you have this feeling that it might come back. Because if you remove it: gone is gone!

On the other hand, every line of HTML comment adds a line to your file and also makes it visible to the world, as every browser has an option to look at the source code. So once you start using a server-side language such as PHP, which you will learn in a few chapters, it is better to place your comments inside that code. You will discover that the syntax for comments in CSS and PHP is different.

As promised, we will now describe the most important HTML tags and attributes, divided in functionality groups. We will start with what started it all: **links**.

Links

In all likelihood, the first web page that was ever created contained a link to the second ever web page. To place a link on a page, we use the anchor tag `<a>`.

The `<a>` tag and attributes

If we simply place some text inside an `<a>` tag, nothing will really happen when you click on it, unless you program the event in JavaScript. However, you can tell from the way it looks on the screen that the intent is for it to be a link. By default, the content of an `<a>` tag is rendered in the (by now probably notorious) underlined and blue style.

```
<a>Click here</a>
```

The href attribute

To make the link work, you need to use the **href** or **hypertext reference** attribute. You can link to another web page, external or local, a document or image, or another section of the current page. Here are some examples:

```
<a href="http://www.packtpub.com">Visit our website</a>
<a href="index.html">Home<//a>
<a href="pdfs/manual.pdf">Click here to download the manual</a>
<a href="#top">Go back to top </a>
```

The first three examples should be self-explanatory. There is a complete URL, a single file name, `index.html`, and a relative path to a PDF file. Absolute pathnames are supported but their use is not recommended. The last example requires more explanation. Did you notice the sharp sign?

The <a> name attribute

The name attribute when used in conjunction with the <a> tag can be used to name a particular spot on the page. That name can then be used elsewhere on the page in a link.

So, you could put this somewhere near the top of your page:

```
<a name="top"></a>    <!-- note that there does not have to be any
content   -->
```

A link somewhere else on the page, using the same name, but preceded with a # sign, will take us back there:

```
<a href="#top">Back to top </a>
```

The <a> target attribute

When a user clicks on a link and arrives at a new page, they sometimes want to go back to where they came from. Some devices and most browsers feature a **back** and even **forward** button a visitor can click on only to discover that the browser does not always take them back to the page they expect. Or the button may not have any effect at all.

In the second half of the book, we will spend an entire chapter on this topic and the notion of what a **previous** page should really be. For now, you can help your cause and your visitor by adding the target attribute to your anchor element. It allows you to determine whether or not the target page (hence the name of the attribute) will open in a new browser window or not. There are four options:

- **target="_blank"**: This page opens up in a new window or tab
- **target="_self"**: This page opens in the same window it was clicked in; this is the default but also sometimes means that you created a point of no return
- **target="_top"**: This page opens in the full window size of the browser
- **target="_parent"**: This page opens in the parent window

Classic document elements

This section lists a few HTML elements that will look familiar to users of word processors or desktop publishing programs.

<h1>, <h2>, <h3>, … <h6> – headings

These are headings. The smaller the number, the larger the font size the browser will render the heading in.

<p> – paragraph

This is the paragraph tag. Browsers automatically add some space (margin) before and after each <p> element. The margins can be modified with CSS (with the margin properties).

<span> – span

The span tag by itself has no visual effect but it is extremely useful when you need to style just a portion of text.

You can use it like this:

```
<h3>Example</h3>
<p>This is a paragraph with one <span
class="blue">blue</span>word</span>
```

Lists

In almost every document, you will find the need to sum up a number of items in a list. In HTML you have the choice between an unordered list (think bullets) and an ordered list (think numbers). The HTML elements for these lists are <ul> and <ol>.

This example produces a list of colors:

```
<h2>Colors</h2>
<ul>
<li>red</li>
<li>green</li>
<li>blue</li>
</ul>
```

This will generate a list of colors, each preceded by a (round) bullet. Replacing `<ul>/</ul>` by `<ol>/</ol>` will give you a numbered list. Attributes existed to specify the shape of the bullet but these are long gone. Bullet styles are specified in CSS these days. You can even use an image file for the bullet.

A third list element that is worth looking into is `<dl>` or data list.

Images

It is hard to imagine a website without images. Most people assume that adding a picture to a site is easy, that it may take a little bit of Photoshopping and that's it. This is actually not true, but it is all manageable. Being a photographer myself, I was disappointed to discover on my first time experimenting with HTML that putting text right next to a picture on a web page was painful. That was because I did not know enough CSS at the time.

There is actually only one HTML element needed to deal with images: the `<img>` tag.

`<img>` element and attributes

A typical piece of HTML containing an image would be:

```
<img  src="images/lupine.jog" alt="lupine" />
```

An `img` tag will never have any content inside so we always use the shorthand notation. The two attributes that are always present are `src` and `alt`. The value of the `alt` attribute is a text that will be displayed when the image file cannot be found or when device is used that cannot display images. The `src` attribute contains the path to the image file. An image file can be in one of many different formats: `.jpeg`, `.gif`, `.png`, `.tiff`, etc.

When no information is given about the actual size of the part of the screen that we want to use to display the image, it will be shown at its actual size, so beware of large image files.

Image width and height

There are two attributes you can use for this: **width** and **height**. This will cause the browser to render the image at the size you specify, but it is far better to not use these attributes at and specify the width and height in CSS. So give your `<img>` tag a class or an `id` tag to do so.

You will later learn that you even have the opportunity to specify different image sizes for different screen sizes when we are discussing **responsive** designs.

Either way, once you know what the largest ever size of the image that is going to be used is, create a version of your image file of exactly those dimensions to use on your site. If the original was larger, you will not force the visitor to download a large file that they do not need. If the original was smaller, create a quality image file at the larger size, so it will look good, rather than you relying on how the browser will extrapolate the image.

Input forms

You have all seen them and used them and now you are going to create them: registration forms, order forms—in short: **forms**. What all forms have in common is that the user will enter, or input, some information. Next, that input is validated— for example, to verify that an e-mail address is actually in the correct format—and then it is processed one way or another.

The form will, of course, be written in HTML and CSS. Validation can happen on the client side before it is processed, in JavaScript, and on the server side while it is processed. The processing is, in most cases, done in PHP and the result stored in some kind of database, such as MySQL or MongoDB, or a non-database, such as a flat file, an XML file, or an Excel spreadsheet. For now, let's focus on the creation of the form itself.

Form elements

The elements we will discuss here to be used in forms are : `<form>`, `<label>`, `<input>`, `<textarea>`, `<button>`, `<select>`, and `<option>`. We will treat `<select>` separately.

This is an example of a typical portion of HTML describing a form:

```
<form id="myform" action"processing.php" method="post"
class="formclass">
<label for="title">Title</label>
<input type="radio" value="Ms" id="title" "name="title"
class="classic">Ms.</input>
<input type="radio" value="Mr" id="title" "name="title"
class="classic">Mr</input>
<label for="first">First Name</label>
<input type="text" name="first" id="first" class="classic" />
<label for="last">Last Name </label>
<input type="text" name="last" id="last" class="classic" />
```

```
<label for="email">email</label>
<input type="text" name="email" id="email" class="classic" />
<button type="submit">Register</button>
</form>
```

Form attributes

Notice the `action` and `method` attributes for the `form` tag. They indicate the name of the program that will be used to process the data and the method used to do so. We will explain this in great detail in *Chapter 5, PHP*.

The label attribute

The `label` element is a useful tag to label the `input` elements. The `for` attribute ties a `label` tag to an `input` tag.

Input attributes

The `input` element is the most versatile element to be used in a form. It is used to let the user give input, either by typing some text or by checking off a checkbox or radio button.

There are several types, specified by the `type` attribute:

Attribute	Description
type="text"	This is the default so there is no need to specify this attribute: this is for text.
type="hidden"	This one does not show, but it is extremely useful to pass values.
type="radio"	This creates a radio button: only one can be selected.
type="checkbox"	This creates a checkbox: multiple checkboxes can be selected.
type="password"	This is like text but the inputted characters are not shown.
type="button"	This creates a button. You can also create buttons using the <button> tag.
type="submit"	This creates a submit button. This means the form will be send to the server. You can also create a submit button using the <button> element and its type="submit" attribute.
type="file"	This creates a file upload dialog with a Choose file button. When you use the multiple attribute and the browser supports it, you can select multiple files.

The name attribute

Every input element that is going to be processed once your visitor has done something with it, needs to have a name. That name will end up being used to create a variable name on the server side when the form is processed. Radio button input elements that belong together should be given the same name.

In the case of the checkbox type input, you should not only use the same name for every checkbox input element, you also want to use square brackets behind the name. The result of this is that you will have access to an array of all the checked elements on the processing side, which will become extremely handy.

The value attribute

This one is used to assign default values to input elements or to assign values that were previously used in the form and were since stored in a database, as would be the case in any kind of "This was your choice, would you like to change anything?" situation.

The checked attribute

Use this when a radio button or checkbox needs to be checked by default.

The readonly attribute

If you specify readonly, the visitor will not be able to enter any input.

Textarea

When input is expected in a form that is longer than just a few words, you can use the textarea element to display an input box. You can specify the size of the box in rows and columns by using the rows and cols attributes. Here is an example:

```
<textarea row="4" cols="50" id="mytextbox">
</textarea>
```

Drop-down lists

Often we need to have visitors make a choice from a list. For this purpose, we can use the `<select>` element in combination with the `<option>` tag for every individual choice. The text portion of the `<option>` element is what will be displayed, and the value of the `value` attribute is what will be passed on for processing. It is very useful to make the first option the one that is not to be chosen, as in the following example:

```
<select name="colorlist" id="colorlist">
<option value="0">Choose a color</option>
<option value="red">Red</option>
<option value="blue">Blue</option>
<option value="green">Green</option>
<option disabled value="orange">Orange</option>
</select>
```

The disabled attribute

Both the `<select>` and the `<option>` support **disabled** in case you want to enable an option (or the entire drop-down list) to be displayed but not selectable.

The selected attribute

If you want to preselect one of the choices, use the **selected** attribute of `<option>`.

Tables

Tables are heavily used in HTML documents. If you want to present data in a grid of columns and rows, like in a spreadsheet, you may want to create a table. A cell in a table can not only contain numbers or words, it can even contain an image or ... another table.

By default, the browser will make a judgment call as to how wide each column will have to be, depending on the width of the cell contents and how much room there is for the table overall.

Table elements

The following HTML elements are used to create tables:

<table>

This is the main tag to create a table. Every table begins with a `<table>` tag and ends with a `</table>` tag.

<thead> <tbody>

These (optional) elements allow you to separate (and subsequently style) the header part and body part of a table. Like in spreadsheets, the header is used for the descriptions of what goes in the table rows, and the body for the actual content. You can use more than one `<tbody>` section to better organize (and style) your table.

<tr>

No rows? No table. The `<tr>` or **table row** is the element you are going to use for all the rows in your table, both the header and body section.

<th> <td>

These are the elements for your table cells. The `<th>` tags are used for your labels in the table header and the `<td>` (table data) for your content cells in the table body.

Table attributes

Some of the table elements have attributes that are unique to tables. We will discuss them here.

colspan (td)

A table that consists of x rows and y columns will of course contain x *times* y cells. With the `colspan` attribute, you can specify that, for a given cell, you want to span it across a number of columns. The following line will span this table cell across three columns:

```
<td colspan="3">Verylongname</td>
```

rowspan (td)

This is the equivalent of `colspan` but for rows. With this attribute, you can specify that you want a table cell to be higher than just a single row.

Let's take a look at a table example:

```
<table>
<thead>
<tr><th>First</th><th>Last</th><th>Organization</th><th>Phone</th></tr>
</thead><tbody>
<tr><td>John</td><td>Muir</td><td>Yosemite</td><td></td></tr>
<tr><td colspan="2">Michael Tilson Thomas</td><td>San Francisco
Symphony</td><td>4158885555</td></tr>
<tr><td>Diane </td><td>Nicolini</td><td rowspan="2">KDFC</td><td
rowspan="2">415888KDFC</td></tr>
<tr><td>Bill</td><td>Lueth</td></tr>
</tbody>
</table>
```

<div>, the "uebertag"

Finally, there is the `<div>`, the tag of all tags. When you run into a problem trying to fit things on the page where you want them, you will most likely solve it by inserting a number of `<div>` elements. Think of a `<div>` as a rectangular section of your page. You can even organize your page as a grid. The framework we will be using in the second half of the book is exactly that. It uses a 12-column grid.

Look at this very simple, yet not uncommon example:

```
<body>
<div id="header"></div>
<div id="container">
<div id="left"></div><div id="middle"></div><div id="right"></div>
</div>
<div id="footer"></div>
</body>
```

Just make this the body of a new HTML page, `minigrid.html`, and look at it. You will see ... nothing, because none of the `<div>` elements have any content, in which case they do not have any size. `<div>` elements are so-called block elements. We will cover this in great detail in the next chapter. Before we do that, we are going to conclude this chapter on HTML with a very important topic: **HTML entities**.

HTML entities

As we know, all tags begin with a < sign and end with a > sign. Just imagine you want to use one of those as part of your content. This just might confuse the browser. That is why we have HTML entities.

HTML entities are strings that begin with an ampersand and end with a semicolon.

- This represents the ampersand itself:

  `&amp;`

- A very useful HTML entity is the non-breaking space:

  ` `

  It allows you to insert one or more spaces in you content. To use the < or > sign in your content, we have: `&lt;` and `&gt;`

- Also very useful are `&eur;`, for the Euro symbol, `&copy;` for the copyright sign, and `&reg;` for the Registered Trademark sign.

- Non-English characters can be represented as HTML entities as well, for example, `&eacute;` for é, `&egrave;` for è, and `&ecirc;` for ê.

We recommend you look up some of the online references if you want to see a complete list.

HTML5-specific tags

HTML5 introduced a number of new tags that can help you to add structure to your document, as they all have the names of common components of a document or site, such as header, footer, or article.

If you have been doing web development for a while, you will have used these names in all likelihood, but as a class to categorize `<div>` elements. So if you used `<div class="header">`, you can now use `<header>`. Or, to turn things around, if you already use `<header>`, your fallback plan to support non-HTML5-capable browsers could contain `<div class="header">`.

Here is a brief overview of what they are and how they can be used:

- `<header>`: This is used to contain the headline for a page or section. It typically contains a company logo and navigational elements.

- `<footer>`: Footers typically contain links to other related information, contact info, and copyright statements. Make sure you keep the latter up-to-date. People will not trust the information on a site that has a date of two years ago.

- `<nav>`: This container can be used for the main navigation portion of your site.

- `<aside>`: This tag is very useful to place the component of your side that often is placed on the left, next to everything else.

- `<article>` and `<section>`: These two are useful to better organize your document. You can use them for blog posts or, as the names suggest, articles or sections.

Summary

In this chapter, you learned the basics of HTML, the first of several languages we will use to do web development. HTML uses tags such as `<div>` and tags can also have attributes, for example, `<p class="blue">blue paragraph</p>`. All these tags combined on a page, an HTML page, form the building blocks of a website. Rather than giving an exhaustive list and description of all available HTML elements of tags, we walked you through the most common and useful ones.

HTML elements are used to add content to a website, not to give the site a certain look. Colors, the background and foreground, letter types, borders around images, and many more visible features of a site are handled through style sheets and another language. That language is CSS and that is the topic of our next chapter.

3
CSS

In the previous chapter, we learned how to create HTML documents using HTML elements and attributes. We can even include images and links to other documents and images. But when you look at the result on a screen, you are probably disappointed. I hope you are, because that was done on purpose (oops, I almost said by design, but the design part is what this chapter is all about). When I wrote my first web pages, I was disappointed too, in particular when discovering how hard it was to do something that should be simple: putting a photograph on a page and some text right next to it. Well now, it's time to turn disappointment into excitement!

In this chapter, we will learn how to add the presentation part—in other words the layout—to our web pages, using **Cascading Style Sheets** (CSS). Style sheets are a common feature in Desktop Publishing software. They allow you to specify (or modify) the style of a section of a certain kind in your document: for example, every paragraph of text. When I developed my first book in Adobe InDesign, I knew exactly what I wanted every component to look like, so I modified the letter type and size of all of them by hand. I did not want to spend the time learning how to create style sheets. I have, however, since regretted that decision as at that point it had become a time-consuming affair.

Today, I love style sheets and not only do I recommend using them but to let them be the first thing that you create when you start a new project. A style sheet is like a plan for a plan, where you can fill out the details later.

By using style sheets you can separate the design part from the content part. You can even have this done at separate times or by separate people and it will give all of your pages a consistent look and feel. Simply switch two style sheets and your entire site will look completely different. Are we excited now?

Let us start with a sample piece of CSS code:

```
/* selector - by the way this is how to do comments in CSS */
p.red
/* properties */
{
color:red;
font-family:baskerville, cambria,  serif;
font-size:12px;
font-style:italic;
}
```

Comments in CSS can be found in-between the strings /* and */ similar to that used within the C programming language. So, to encourage good behavior, we included some comments in our first example. Let's analyze the rest of this code.

The part before the curly brace is called the **selector**. It represents one or several elements in our page. In our example, that would include all <p> elements with class red.

In-between the curly braces, we find the CSS rules we want. In this example, we want all text inside paragraphs to be red, size 12 pixels, in italics, and in the **Baskerville** typeface. On systems where that font is not available, we want **Cambria** to be used instead.

Note that every rule ends with a *semicolon* and consists of two parts separated by a colon: a **property** and a **value**. Color is a property and in our example the value chosen is red.

In old versions of HTML, the same could have been achieved by placing <font> elements inside your <p> tags. Imagine having 40 <p> sections in your document and someone wants to change the red into maroon! You would have to change your HTML file in 40 different places, and no- a global find and replace would not even help you, as there might be other red "things". By using CSS, you only need to change one line.

It is more common to find CSS code similar to this one:

```
p {
font-size:12px;
font-family:Baskerville,cambria, serif;
}
p.red {
font-style:italic;
color:red;
}
```

This will not only have the same effect for red `<p>` s , but it will also put all other paragraphs in the same typeface and size. This is the C in CSS: the properties of the overall `<p>` flows into the subset of red ones, like in a real cascade.

Adding styles to our documents

So how do the CSS rules become part of our document? There are three ways:

- External style sheets
- Internal CSS
- Inline styles

External style sheets

This is the recommended way to add CSS to your site. It should be your goal for all style sheets of the production version of your site to be external. Simply add a line to the `<head>` section of your site, which should look like the following:

```
<link rel="stylesheet" type="text/css" href="css/style.css">
```

`<link>` is an HTML element we had not yet introduced. Its attributes are listed below:

- `rel`, to indicate the relationship between the HTML document and the linked file.

- `type` specifies the MIME type of the document so the browser knows how to load it.

- `href` is used to specify the location of the file. You may expect a `src` attribute here, like is used for `<img>` tags, but the attribute to specify the file name in a `<link>` element is `href`. For the file name, we recommend that you always use relative pathnames. We suggest that you collect all your style sheets together in a folder with a meaningful name, like `css` or `styles`. Of course, the file itself should have a meaningful name too.

When the file does indeed exist, it will be loaded. That is why it is important that your `<link>` element resides in the `<head>` section of the document so all the CSS rules are read before the body of your document.

Internal CSS

For small projects, or projects you would like to limit to a single HTML file so that it is easy to email to someone, you can use internal CSS. All the CSS rules can then be placed inside the `<head>` section of your document, inside a `<style>` tag. That tag needs to, at a minimum, include a `type` attribute, as in the following example:

```
<style type="text/css">
p.red {
color:red;
}
</style>
```

Inline styles

Styles can be given to an individual HTML element by using the `style` attribute inside the HTML element itself, as in the following example:

```
<h3 style="color:green;">Congratulations</h3>
```

We do not recommend using this in your final product, but it is extremely useful to instantly see the effect of a change during development. If, for some reason, you leave one of the inline style attributes inside a page, it might take you forever to find out why your cool style sheet is not doing what it is supposed to be doing, on this one line of this one page.

On the other hand, I use it everyday, as I introduce and test new elements on a page while not disturbing anything else on the site, as modifying the external `.css` file would.

The Document Object Model (DOM)

As we learned in the previous chapter, an HTML document consists of a tree structure of nested tags, with HTML as the root. In programming, the contents of that tree can be stored in a large object and subtrees can be accessed, modified, or added by using smaller objects.

The whole lot is referred to as the **Document Object Model** (**DOM**). In subsequent chapters, we will learn a programming language (JavaScript) to do exactly that and a JavaScript library (jQuery) to make it easier. In this chapter, we will not be learning how to change our content, but we will learn how to change the style of our content. In all cases, we need a way to access our document. This is where **selectors** fit in.

Selectors

The first part of a CSS rule, the part before the opening curly brace, is the selector, or several selectors separated by commas. A selector represents a *collection* of elements in the page to which the subsequent rules apply. The simplest selector is a single tag name, such as the one we already used in a previous example. Following is a code snippet as another example:

```
p {
color:blue;
}
```

The selector p means all paragraph elements in the entire page. Applying this rule will result in all paragraphs in the entire page being rendered in blue. Similarly, we could use a class name. Refer to the following example:

```
.blue {
color:blue;
}
```

The selector .blue represents all the elements in the page that have the class blue, whether they are paragraphs, headings, or so on. Now we can combine the two, as shown here:

```
p.blue {
color:blue;
}
```

This selector represents the collection of all paragraph elements on the page with the class set to blue. For those of you that like set theory, this is the intersection of the p collection and the .blue collection.

Let's go for some more set theory in the next simple example:

```
#errorbox {
color:red;
}
```

The set of elements that matches this selector is, at best, a singleton, as it matches the element with its **id** set to errorbox, if present. I cannot remind you often enough that no two elements can share the same id. Equally valid, but slightly more restrictive, is the following rule:

```
div#errorbox {
color:red;
}
```

The former rule was about any element with an id `errorbox`: the latter only applies to a `div` element with the id `errorbox`.

Multiple classes

We learned that several different classes can be assigned to an element by assigning a space separated string to its `class` attribute, for example:

```
class="green cool awesome"
```

If you want to create a CSS rule for an element like this, the selector could look like the following:

```
h2.green.cool.awesome
```

When used as a selector in a CSS rule, the rule would apply to all `h2` elements of class `green`, as well as `cool` and `awesome`. So the style would be changed to the following:

```
<h2 class="green cool awesome">The Hulk</h2>
```

This is completely different from a rule with the following selector:

```
h2   .green .cool .awesome
```

This would be part of a rule applying to elements that have the class `awesome`, are descendant of elements with the class `cool`, which are in turn descendants of tags with the class set to `green`, while being themselves a descendant of an `h2` element.

This is a very important distinction, so it is very important to remember: if you allow me to paraphrase a famous song: *What a difference a space makes*!

Descendants

The sample selectors we used so far are all top level selectors: an element, a class, or an identifier. Now we are going to add more detail, and more complexity. Look at the following example:

```
#container h2 {
color:grey;
}
```

This rule applies only to the `h2` elements that are inside an element with the `id="container"`, no matter how many levels deep they are. So if this was a chunk of your HTML file, the rule would apply to the `h2` element that contains it:

```
<div id="container">
<div id="header"></div>
```

```
<div id="main">
<h2>Title of this Document </h2>
</div>
</div>
```

The following CSS rule will make the heading `grey` as well, but if by any chance there are other `h2` elements inside the `#header` div, they would not be affected by this rule:

```
#container #main h2 {
color:grey;
}
```

Selecting children or siblings

In some cases, you want to be more specific in your selection and have a rule for elements that are the **children** of other elements, not descendants of arbitrary numbers of differing levels down in the document tree. For this purpose you can use the **child selector**, as in the following example:

```
#main >  h2 {
color:grey;
}
```

`h2` is a child of the div element with the id `main`, so with this rule also, the heading in our little chunk of code will be displayed in `grey`. Now consider the following example: On the other hand:

```
#container > h2 {
color:grey;
}
```

In this case, there will be no effect as `h2` is not a child of `div#container`.

There is a similar syntax for specifying an element that is adjacent to another one, or a **sibling** as this would be called in a family tree. Refer to the next example:

```
h2 + p  {
margin-top:0px;
}
```

This would not give a top margin to a p element that immediately follows a `h2`, but would not apply this rule to subsequent p tags. Look at the following small piece of HTML:

```
<h2>Story</h2>
<p>First paragraph</p>
```

```
<p>Second paragraph</p>
<p>Third paragraph</p>
```

The first paragraph would not have a top margin; all others would have margins based on how the browser renders the paragraphs by default. Of course, this is true if this CSS rule is the only one and not overruled by others, and this brings us to the next topic: **specificity**.

Specificity

From time to time, as a CSS beginner or an experienced web developer, you will be frustrated if you just added a new CSS rule to your style sheet and discovered that it has no effect. More often than not, this happens because there is another rule with a higher specificity that has priority.

We already mentioned that inline styles take precedence over external style sheets. So it seems more than logical that the order of internal CSS and links to external style sheets will influence how the page will end up looking. Now consider the following rule:

```
p.warning {
color:red;
}
```

Suppose the previous stated rule is followed by this next rule:

```
p.warning {
color:orange;
}
```

In such a scenario, all paragraph elements with the class warning will appear in orange, not red, because the orange rule appeared later.

But these two rules happen to share a common selector: it is a p with the class warning.

Things would be different if you had rules with selectors such as the following:

```
p#error {
color:red;
}
```

And along with that, if you also had the next rule:

```
body div.container div.main p.error {
color: orange;
}
```

Let us now consider the following:

```
<div class="container">
<div class="main">
<p id="error" class="error">
What you typed is incorrect
</p>
</div></div>
```

Logic or intuition, but not the order in the CSS, would make us think that the text What you typed is incorrect would be displayed in red and not in orange. This is, in fact, correct, but we do not want to rely on intuition, do we? Fortunately, there are formulas to determine which CSS rule wins if there are several that could influence the layout of a particular element. It is slightly mathematical and referred to as **specificity**.

The specificity of a CSS rule is a sequence of four numbers that are calculated as follows:

- If the rule is an inline style, the first number is 1, otherwise it is 0
- Add 1 to the second number for every occurrence of an **identifier**
- Add 1 to the third number for every **class** specified
- Increase the fourth number by one for every **element** present

When two rules are compared, the first number is looked at first. If one of them is higher, then that rule has more **weight**. Next, the second number is looked at, and if needed, the third, and finally the last. The specificity of our two sample rules is: 0,1,0,1 and 0,0,3,4.

So our intuition is now confirmed by mere arithmetic.

Block elements and inline elements

Before we finally get into a description of the most important CSS properties by category, we need to say a few words on two categories of elements: **block** elements and **inline** elements.

Think of block elements as rectangular areas of your screen or page. They can contain text, data, and other block elements, as well as inline elements. Typical block elements are the <div> and <p> tags. Before and after every block element, a new line of text is created.

Inline elements can only contain inline elements and not block elements. Also, they cannot be given a width. They inherit the width from the container that they are inside of. The most popular inline element is the <span> element, typically used to change the look of a chunk of text inside more text.

For starters this can be confusing, because block elements like <div> may be block elements, but when they have no content inside of them, they appear not to have any width or height. Moreover, you can change the way these elements are displayed with the CSS display property. Consider the following lines of code and have a browser render it:

```
<p>paragraph1</p>
<p>paragraph2</p>
<p>paragraph3</p>
<p>paragraph4</p>

<p style="display:inline;">paragraph1</p>
<p style="display:inline;">paragraph2</p>
<p style="display:inline;">paragraph3</p>
<p style="display:inline;">paragraph4</p>
```

The first four lines are displayed as block elements and are true paragraphs: there will be a new line in-between them, and the distance between these paragraphs will be determined by the default font and margin values the browser has chosen. Font and margin belong to the most important CSS property families. We will learn about them when we discuss the font properties and the so called box model for margin, border, and padding.

The second set of paragraphs will all appear on one line, if permitted by room in the viewport, because we explicitly declared them to be inline elements.

Before we discuss the box model, let us look at one more example. Experiment with the first half set of divs as it will, as is, display nothing. Once you insert text in between the <div> tags, that text will appear along with the background colors. The <div> elements in the second set actually have a width and height, so you will see four perfect colorful squares, but maybe not the way you expected them. We grouped them two by two, yet they all appear stacked on top of each other. Welcome to the world of browser indifference!

```
<style type="text/css">
.redbg {
background-color: red;
}
.greenbg {
background-color: green;
```

```
}
.yellowbg {
background-color: yellow;
}
.bluebg {
background-color: blue;
}
.sq200 {
width: 200px;
height: 200px;
}
</style>

<div>
<div class="redbg"></div><div class="yellowbg"></div>
</div>
<div>
<div class="greenbg"></div><div class="bluebg"></div>
</div>

<div>
<div class="sq200 redbg"></div><div class="sq200 yellowbg"></div>
</div>
<div>
<div class="sq200 greenbg"></div><div class="sq200 bluebg"></div>
</div>
```

Colors

What can make a site look instantly more pleasant is the proper use of colors. It is also a useful tool for doing some debugging. By adding different background colors to some block elements, you are increasing your chances of finding the location of that one missing, closing tag that messes things up. I just used it today.

There is a world of difference between publishing printed books, documents, and even packaging components or media faceart through a professional manufacturing company, and web publishing. In the world of printing, you have full control over the colors you use and, also extremely critical, the fonts or typefaces. You should be very exigent and expect the resulting product to match exactly in color and typeface to what you specified. Color information is exchanged in either RGB (**red-green-blue**) or CMYK (**cyan-magenta-yellow-black**) values. In CSS also, you can specify the desired color through its RGB values. But this is where the comparison begins and ends.

Because of this, we know that colors of a quality printed item should look exactly the way we expect them to. However, when we prepare web content, we cannot tell how the colors on our site will look to our visitors. It depends on too many things. For example, what device do they use: a computer, a tablet, or a mobile phone? The screen they look at can be large or small, be of high or low resolution, and support millions of colors or just a small number. Once we realize that, we are fine. I therefore recommend using colors that are sufficiently distinct, and to not bother using extravagant RGB combinations.

Colors can be specified in several ways. The two most common ones are by **name** and by **RGB** value. Names are easier, but may be more subject to browser interpretation. So I only use them for quick and temporary things, or when they are *black* or *white*. In all other cases, I prefer to use the RGB values, which are written as the # sign followed by three two digit hex numbers, for example, `#FFDEAD`, one of my favorite colors. It is called **Navajo**.

You can use colors for the foreground and the background, with the **color** and **background-color** properties. Color indicates the color that will be used to display the text inside an element or the descendants of an element; background-color, as the property name suggests, will set the background color of a block element.

Fonts

I am a typography enthusiast. I even spent money buying fonts, just for personal use. So I would like to point out that, even more so than with colors, there is a huge difference between using typography for print publishing and web publishing.

In print publishing, you are in full control of `fonts` or `typefaces` (this is not a typography book, so allow me to use these terms interchangeably) that you use in your work. You just have to make sure that all the fonts that you plan to use are installed on the system that holds your `Desktop Publishing` program, so you can use them for your development. Next, make sure that they are **embedded** in the final document you send to your printer, and that both you and your printing company have a legitimate license for all the fonts used. Then all the people who will read the printed copy or even a PDF version online, will see it just the way you designed it.

When publishing on the web, the text that the visitor will see on your page can only be displayed in a font that is actually installed on the device he or she is using. The worst case, yet the best looking, scenario is the one where you use a very nice, expensive font that is installed on the system used to design and test your site. It is possible that is it installed on no other computer on the planet.

That website will look absolutely fabulous on your own computer but potentially dreadful where it matters most. That is why in CSS we work with **font families**, and not single fonts.

Before getting into more detail, one thing to note about the web **middle ages**, is that there used to be a tag `<font>` — simply think — ah! middle ages and do not use it. It is one of those presentational HTML elements we talked about.

So what are fonts?

In simple terms, fonts are a series of pictures, or **glyphs**, determining how letters, numbers, and other characters should be displayed. In the early days of printing, some 500 years ago, Gutenberg, Plantijn, or Moretus created metal casts, one letter at a time. These metal letters would be placed in wooden cases, the larger ones in the upper and the smaller in the lower case. This is how the terms uppercase and lowercase were born.

To compose a single page of text, metal letters had to be put in a frame to hold them together and then inserted in the world's first printing press. Add some ink and paper and there you had it: you had one page of one copy of a book. Of course, for every different size, thickness, and style (for example *italic* versus *normal*), there had to be a separate case with letters.

The people who created those metal letters were called punch-cutters and the fonts were named after them. A famous one was Claude Garamond. You can spot the original Garamond metal fonts, wrapped in paper to protect for posterity, at the Plantijn-Moretus Museum in Antwerp (it is my favorite museum in Belgium). You will discover there that the 16th century equivalent of a combined architect, portraitist, and "web designer" was Peter Paul Rubens, known to most other people only as a painter.

Today, the fonts we talk about are no longer small blocks of metal, but computer files with information on the font layout. The more glyph collections a font contains (more sizes, styles, or weight or thickness), the more accurately a letter will be reproduced.

Font families

Fonts can be divided into different categories or families. The three most important ones are called **serif**, **sans-serif** and **monospace** fonts.

Serif fonts

Serif fonts are typefaces that have glyphs with small decorations or serifs at some of the edges of the letter. For example, the short lines at the bottom of each leg in the letter *m*.

The font designed by Garamond, mentioned in the previous section, is an example of a serif font. Serif fonts are popular because they make reading text pleasant. Publishers use well crafted serif fonts, combined with high quality printing paper, in the hardcover versions of their books. **Times New Roman**, designed for a British newspaper The Times, is a very commonly used serif font. The very text you are now reading is in Times New Roman. The creators used a font called Plantin as a model, which in turn was named after **Plantijn,** the printer person I mentioned earlier.

Baskerville is another example of a serif font and is used a lot for eBooks.

Using serif fonts for the text portion of a website is subject to discussion. As glyphs have to be displayed using pixels on a screen, the decorations that cause a pleasant read in print may result in just the opposite on a screen,. This is because on lower resolution screens, those same decorations may look too pixilated. I personally recommend at least experimenting with some serif fonts for the main text part of your site before making that call.

Sans-serif fonts

Sans-serif fonts are the counterpart of serif fonts. They do not contain the small decorations or serifs at the end of the stroke, hence the name sans (French for without) serif. In print, sans-serif fonts are used for headings, titles, and so on. This is in contrast to the serif fonts used for the body of the text. Sans-serif fonts, for the reason mentioned previously, are now more common for text that needs to be displayed on computer screens. Common sans-serif typefaces are: **Arial**, **Open Sans,** and **Helvetica**. Headings in this book are in Arial.

Monospace fonts

In the typefaces we have discussed so far, not all characters have the same width: the letter m is clearly wider than the letter i. A monospaced font, also called a fixed-width, is a font where letters and characters do indeed have the same width. The first monospaced typefaces were for typewriters, as the carriage always moves the same distance forward with each letter typed. They were also used in early computers and computer terminals. Software text editors still use them today, as it makes it easier to align source code when every character has the same width.

The source code displayed on web sites is usually displayed in a monospace font, as are the code examples in this book. The most common monospace font is probably **Courier**. Another example is **Lucida Console**.

Let us now get back from our trip into the science and the history of typography, to our CSS story.

The font-family property

To specify how the text of an element needs to be displayed, we use the **font-family** property in the CSS style sheet. For example, consider the following:

```
p {
font-family: "Open Sans", "Helvetica Neue", Verdana, Helvetica, sans-
serif;
}
```

So why is there more than one font specified: a letter can only be in one font, can't it?

This is how it works. When someone visits your site, with this sentence in your style sheet, a paragraph of text will be displayed in the Open Sans typeface, if it is installed on the visitor's computer. If it is not found, Helvetica Neue will be looked for; if that one is not there then Verdana is attempted, and so on. If everything fails, some default sans-serif typeface will be used. For this example, the last scenario is very unlikely, as I cannot imagine a system that would not have Verdana or Helvetica installed. Yet, it is recommended to always conclude the list with sans-serif, serif, or monospace. Note the use of quotes (For example, for 'Helevtica Neue') when font names consist of more than one word.

Font-weight and font-style

When you select a font using one of the desktop applications you use, you can also select style from picklist. A typical picklist could include: normal, italic, semi-bold, semi-bold italic, bold, and bold italic. The number of items on that list typically matches the number of glyph collections that came with the font. You can visit a website of a company that sells fonts, to get a better feel for how many variations there can be on the theme of a single font.

In CSS, the equivalent of this is provided through two different properties: **font-weight** and **font-style**.

The two most common values for font-style are **normal** and **italic**. The ones for font-weight are **normal** and **bold**, and the numbers 100, 200, and so on, through 900. 400 is the same as normal and 700 the same as bold. All others can have unpredictable results depending on the presence of, let's say, a semi-bold version of your font and the browser used. So until we reach the second part of the book, the message should be loud and clear—only use the basic normal or italic, and normal or bold.

Font-size

Finally, as in our desktop applications, we can specify now which font our text needs to be displayed in, and what size all these letters should have.

Size can be specified in pixels, percentages, or ems. Another one that exists is called rem.

When no font-size is specified anywhere, a typical browser will set that size to 16px. The em unit, a term that comes from typography to refer to the size of the letter m in a font, is, in CSS, nothing other than the calculated size of the font for the current element. Its use is highly recommended over fixed pixel sizes. Let's illustrate this with an example. Look at the following CSS code:

```
h1 {
font-family: "open Sans", Arial, sans-serif;
font-size:2em;
font-weight:bold;
}
h2 {
font-family:Arial, sans-serif;
color:#999999;
font-size:1.5em;
font-weight:600;
}
```

If no font-size was specified for the body element, we know that this would be 16px, with all descendants inheriting it. This means that our h1 heading would become 32px and the h2 would be 24px. Simply changing the font-size for the body element to, let us say, 20px would proportionally change the sizes of our h2 and h1 headings to 30px and 40px respectively. If we had given them a size of, for example, 20px and 24px we would have ended up with headings the same size as the font used for regular text.

The same is true when the user uses the browser to zoom in or zoom out. We retain the proportions. In the interests of creating responsive designs, using proportional sizes rather than fixed ones is the way to go. Of course you have to be careful and realize that when you change the font-size of an element, all children will inherit it, and when you change that, by mistake or not, of a child element, the size of em will no longer be what it was a minute ago.

Consider the following code:

```
<div class="insert">
<p> A paragraph of text that represents what could be an insert in a
book</p>
</div>
```

Following are the CSS rules to go with it:

```
div.insert {
font-family:Baskerville, "Times News Roman", serif;
font-size:0.8em;
color:brown;
}
.insert p {
font-size:0.8em;
}
```

You have just made the font-size twice as small, so that the letters in this paragraph of text will be 0.64.

In general, I like using percentages, as shown next:

```
.insert p {
font-size:80%;
}
```

Line-height

There is one more important property for dealing with text: the **line-height**. In practice, this determines how much vertical space there will be between two lines of text. Line-height can be specified as a number, which is multiplied with the font size, a pixel value, a percentage, or the word normal. Normal is typically determined by the browser and is usually somewhere between 1.2 and 1.4. So the height of every line is 1.2 or 1.4 times the font size. That way there is some room for white space above and below the letters.

For a font with size `16px`, the following three lines of CSS would have the same effect:

```
p {
line-height: 24px;
}
p {
line-height: 1.5;
}

p{
line-height: 150%;
}
```

Note that this specifies the space between lines of a paragraph, not the space between paragraphs. That would be determined by the margin, and the margin is one aspect of the single most important concept of CSS: the **box model**.

The box model

All HTML elements can be treated as boxes. In CSS, the term box model is used while talking about design and layout. It is essentially a box that wraps around HTML elements and that can consist of, from outside to inside: margins, borders, padding, and the actual content.

So far in this book, we have given only short examples so that you could study away from a computer, and we will treat this as a textbook for as long as we can. However, to illustrate the box model, and for you to understand it, it is essential to take our examples and check them in a browser. Consider the following code:

```
<!DOCTYPE html>
<html>
<head>
<meta charset="UTF-8" />
<title>Paul Wellens - California anecdotes</title>
<link rel="stylesheet" href="styles/packtpubch3_1.css"
type="text/css" />
</head>
<body>
<div id="box">
June Lake, often called the gem of the Eastern Sierra, is a beautiful
place that I visit as often as I can.
</div>
<div id="box2">
```

```
Mono Lake, saltier than the Black Sea, features tufa formations that
makes the place look like it could be on the moon
</div>
</div>
</body>
</html>
```

And next is the content of the style sheet file, where we use some of what we just learned, combined with introducing all the box model properties:

```
body {
font-size:12px;
background-color: #ffdead;
font-family:Arial, Verdana, Helvetica, sans-serif;
color:#999;
line-height:1.3;
margin:0;

}

#box {
  width:150px;
  height:150px;
  background-color:teal;
  color:white;
  border: 5px solid orange;
  margin:40px;
  padding:20px;


}
#box2 {
  width:150px;
  height:150px;
  background-color:blue;
  color:white;
  border: 5px solid yellow;
  margin:40px;
  padding:20px;

  }
```

When we display this is in a browser, we will see two square boxes nicely stacked on top of each other. Both boxes have text in them; one is colored green with an orange border, the other one blue and yellow. There is an equal distance between the left of the viewport and the boxes, the top of the window and the top box, and in-between the boxes. Feel free to change the values in the CSS and the HTML of box #box and see what happens.

We have our content where our text goes, which we have specified as 150 by 150 pixels. If we had not specified width and height, we would have ended up with a thick, green rectangular area with text and border across our viewport. If we remove only border and padding, we just see the text with a background-color; if we only remove the text, we see a bordered, colored rectangle; and if we remove both, we end up seeing nothing. Finally, if you put just the width and height back, we have a green square of exactly 150 x 150 pixels.

So starting from the inner side, we have our content with a *specified* or *calculated* size. That is the size of our element: 150 by 150 pixels in our example.

Next we can have **padding**. This takes the same background-color as the element and increases the inner portion of our box. In our example, 20px are added on all four sides of the element.

Then we can have a **border**. This puts a border around our element with the thickness, color, and shape we specify. We used a solid border of 5px around all the sides, and thus, so far our box is already (5 + 25 + 150 + 25 + 5 = 210) x 210 pixels.

Finally, there is the **margin**. The margin, if we want one, is the area on the outer side of our element box. It is transparent, so it has the background color of the parent element. It merely creates a distance between the box and the adjacent box(es). In this example, we used a margin of 40px. This makes the total size of our box (40 + 210 + 40 = 290) x 290 pixels.

If you try this out and are an attentive kind of person, you may notice something that does not compute. Good catch! We will explain this in a little while. We will now go over all the box model properties you can use.

Padding

You can specify, or not, padding on all four sides of your element. For this purpose, there are four properties you can use:

- padding-top
- padding-right

- padding-bottom
- padding-left

Here is an example:

```
.menulabel
{
padding-left: 8px;
padding-right: 7px;
padding-top: 4px;
padding-bottom: 5px;
}
```

Did you notice that I changed the order? I did that on purpose. The first order I used is the one supported by the shorthand version of the `padding` property. The second one is the order I think about when I do my design: what is it horizontally, next vertically. So, the same four lines of CSS can be replaced by the following single one:

```
.menulabel {
padding: 4px 7px 5px 8px;
}
```

In the first example we used a single value, which means four times the same. There are also two and three value variants of the shorthand version as well. For example, the following will set both top and bottom to `10px`, and left and right to `15px`:

```
.menulabel {
padding: 10px 15px;
}
```

Border

For the border property also, you have the option to specify different values for top, right, bottom, and left, but there is more than just the width. You can also specify the shape, style, and the color. So, following are the properties for all three:

- **border-width**
- **border-style**
- **border-color**

There is even a property you can use for any of these three in any direction, such as **border-top-style**, so there are many properties to choose from- not that having so many would be practical. I do not believe a border with a different shape, color, and size on each side would make for a nice design!

The most common shapes or styles to choose from are:

- **none**
- **solid**
- **double**

There are, of course, more. Double gives you a double border and can be quite decorative at times. Solid is what I recommend you use most of the time.

```
myimg {
5px solid white;
}
```

So why would you need none? If I do not want a border, I just do not specify one, right? *Wrong!* Some browsers, such as Internet Explorer, automatically put a white border of 1px around any img element. So be glad you have the option to deal with that:

```
img {
border:none;
}
```

We already used the shorthand notation in our examples, so I only have to remind you of the order of things to include; I constantly forget them myself: **width style color**.

Having the ability to put borders around things is a very cool feature, in particular for photographs. The web equivalent of the "mat" part of a matted photograph can simply be a well-crafted border for the img element.

Margin

Finally, there is the margin property, which clears an element around its borders. It has no background color because it is transparent. The five properties are:

- margin
- margin-top
- margin-right
- margin-bottom
- margin-left

You can specify margin sizes in pixels, in percentages, and so on, just like you can with padding. However, there is one extra, extremely useful value you can set the margin to: **auto**. Change the margin setting in our example to:

```
margin: 40px auto;
```

Like magic, your two square boxes will be centered horizontally. If you make your browser window smaller or bigger, they will still be centered. With the margin set to auto, the browser will calculate the left and right margin for you, relative to the parent element. Many websites have a main `div`, child of the body element, styled similar to the following:

```
#container {
margin: 0px auto;
border:none;
max-width:980px;
}
```

Classical web development uses a canvas with a fixed width, and often fixed height as well, to place everything inside. This example uses `980px`. Thanks to the `auto` margin, there will be an automatic margin on left and right, calculated as half of the remaining horizontal space. The `max-width` is new and differs from `width`. Width will always give you 980 px, max-width only when 980 horizontal pixels are available. If that is not the case, on smartphones for instance, the (smaller) full width of the viewport will become the width. This is one tiny step towards **responsive design**.

Collapsing margins

You have been learning about the box model, have used our example, and may have been wondering why two square boxes with top and bottom margins of 40px are only `40`, not 80 pixels apart.

Well, this is not a bug, but a feature. The W3C specification stipulates that when the vertical margins of two elements are touching, the larger of the two will take effect and the other one is reduced to 0. Some other CSS settings can change this, but this is the default. Once you have done a lot of web development and have gotten used to it, you may decide that it actually makes a lot of sense. We will finish this section by adding two more boxes, with pictures inside of them, to our HTML and CSS, basically creating the first two entries of a photo gallery. We will incorporate what we have learned and discover what is still missing.

Here is the HTML:

```
<!DOCTYPE html>
<html>
<head>
<meta charset=utf-8" />
<title>Paul Wellens - California pictures</title>
```

```
<link rel="stylesheet" href="styles/packtpubch3_photo.css" type="text/
css">
</head>
<body>
<div class="entry">
<div class="picturebox">
<img  class="picture" src=http://www.paulpwellens.com/packtpub/images/
junelakefall.jpg alt="junelake" />
</div>
<div class="textbox">
June Lake, often called the gem of the Eastern Sierra, is a beautiful
place that I visit as often as I can.
</div>
</div>

<div class="entry" >
<div class="picturebox">
<img class="picture" src="http://www.paulpwellens.com/packtpub/images/
monolake.png" alt="monolake" />
</div>
<div class="textbox">
Mono Lake, saltier than the Black Sea, features tufa formations that
makes the place look like it could be on the moon
</div>
</div>
</body>
</html>
```

Put the following in your stylesheet:

```
.picture {
  width:200px;
  height:130px;
  border:5px solid white;
  margin-left:25px;
  margin-top:40px;

}
.entry {

  width:600px;
  margin:0 auto;

}
.picturebox {
```

```
    background-color:teal;
    color:white;
    width:270px;
    height:220px;
    text-align:center;
    vertical-align:middle;
    /* float:left;   */
    border-bottom:1px solid #FFDEAD;

}
.textbox {

    background-color:teal;
    color:white;
    width:250px;
    height:180px;
    padding:40px 10px 0px 10px;
    /* float:left; */
    border-bottom:1px solid #FFDEAD;
    text-align:left;
}
```

If you run this example in a browser, you will notice that despite wrapping them with another div tag, the pictures and the text that goes with it are still not side by side, but stacked on top of each other. The solution is already there, but placed inside the /* and */ string as a comment. Uncomment those lines, and like magic everything will look the way you want it to.

Positioning

There are several CSS properties you can use to alter the position of an element on the page. The one with clearly the most impact is called **float** (each time I use it, it reminds me of the clown character in the Stephen King novel and movie *It!* when it says: *And they all float!*)

Float

I interpret the CSS float property as the CSS way to stack elements horizontally. If you give all of them a:

```
float:left;
```

You stack them from left to right. With a:

```
float:right;
```

You stack them from right to left. This can become very handy when you want to put the first part of your page, an introduction for example, on the right if room is available, and on top if not. In our above example, changing the float left into a float right will put the pictures on the right.

position:relative

The CSS **position** property can be used to position elements in a spot on the page that is different to where they would normally go. "Normally" is the same as position:static. Look at the following code:

```
#redsquare
{
width:100px;
height:100px;
background-color:red;
}
```

This produces a red square in the upper-left corner of its parent element. Now, try the following:

```
#redsquare
{
position:relative;
width:100px;
height:100px;
background-color:red;
left:10px;
top:100px;
}
```

The red square moves 100px down and 10px to the right.

position:absolute

Let's add:

```
#container
{
  width:700px;
  margin:50px;
  background-color:teal;
  height:500px;
}
```

and

```
<body>
<div id="container">
<div id="redsquare">

</div>
</div>
</body>
```

The red square box is now inside the teal box, 100px down, and 10px to the right. When you replace relative by **absolute**, the red box will be 100px down and 10px to the right, relative to the ancestor element instead. This is typically the browser window itself.

Styling lists

One element that you will end up using a lot is the `<ul>` tag: the unordered list. By default, every item in the list will be shown with a round bullet in front of the text. With CSS, you can change the style of your list.

list-style-type

Using this property, you can change the shape of the bullet. Some of the values you can use are: none (no bullet at all), square (a square), circle (a small circle), or disc (the default).

list-style-image

You can provide your own image for the bullet by using the **list-style-image** property. The default value is none, which means that the bullet image is determined by the value of **list-style-type**. However if you specify url, followed by a path to an image, that image will be used instead, for example:

```
url('smiley.gif')
```

list-style-position

By default, the bullets appear outside the content flow. If you specify inside as the value of **list-style-position**, the bullets will move to the inside and the text more to the right.

Styling anchors – pseudo-classes

We conclude our selection on CSS properties with the introduction of some pseudo-classes, typically but not solely used with <a>, the **anchor** tag. The anchor tag is used mainly for links. To make it visible that they are indeed links, the default styling of <a> happens to be a blue color and the text is underlined, which is not very attractive.

Using pseudo-classes, you can give an anchor tag, in theory any tag, a different look depending on where the cursor is, relative to the link and whether or not the link has already been visited. Here is an example:

```
a:link {
text-decoration:none;  /* switches off the underline */
}
a:hover {
color:white;   /* changes color to white when the curser hangs over it
(hover)   */
}
a:visited {
color:yellow;   /* changes the color to indicate that you already
visited that link */
}
```

Firebug

No matter how well you studied this chapter and various online references about CSS, from time to time things will not look as expected. This is where a debugging tool like **Firebug** comes in handy. Firebug is an extension to the Firefox browser. It lets you click on parts of your page, and then the program will show you the HTML and CSS that is involved and even a picture of the box model showing the padding, border, and margin. Most other browsers, Safari and Chrome in particular, have comparable counterparts.

Summary

In this chapter, we gave you an overview of CSS. This is not a complete reference but we did include the most frequently used and useful CSS properties that should be supported by all browsers. We did not include (on purpose) some of the newer ones that were introduced in CSS3. One important new CSS feature that will be introduced in the second part of this book will be **media queries**. This is essential for building responsive designs, but this topic earns at least one chapter of its own.

So far, we have learned two languages we need to create websites: HTML and CSS. Without further delay, we now move on to the next one, a true programming language: **JavaScript**.

4
JavaScript

So far we have gone through three chapters and learned two languages, HTML and CSS. They are used to create a web page, give it content, and add styling to it. In this chapter, we will learn a third language, **JavaScript**, which is used for programming your web pages and add life to them. For quite some time, JavaScript was treated by some as a second class citizen. If ever this was deserved, it is definitely no longer true today. Before we get started with JavaScript, let us get oriented in the world of programming.

Programming 101

There is no such thing as a smart computer. A computer is a device that is capable of executing just a few instructions, but can do that very fast. One such instruction could be to take a value stored somewhere, and another stored somewhere else, add the two, and store the result in a third place. A **program** is a list of such instructions, written down in some logical and structured order, and in a human readable format. The format is called a **programming language**. A smart program would turn the useless device we described into a calculator.

For a lot of programming languages, a special program called a **compiler** exists. It translates a program from a human readable format—usually a text file referred to as source code—into a format the computer can understand, typically a binary executable file.

Your computer or tablet contains many different kinds of programs. There is a program to manage the computer, programs to manage programs, others to create programs, a program that lets you type in commands which in turn are names of programs, and so on. That last one happens to be a programming language too, sometimes called a **shell** or **command interpreter**.

If you put some commands together in a text file, you have once again a program: a shell script. This is an example of a language that is interpreted, not compiled.

But this is *Programming 101*, not Computer 101. Look at the following lines of source code, written in an imaginary programming language:

```
a = 1;
b = 2;
c = a + b;
printnumber (c);
```

The letters a, b, and c are variables — things that can hold values. Those values can be numbers, names, complete employee records, and so on, as well as the value of an expression that contains more variables and values. You find those on the right-hand side of the = sign, which is an **operator**. This operator assigns what is on the right to be the value of the variable on the left. + is also an operator. As you may have guessed, it adds two things. Variables have to be declared first, telling whomever or whatever is going to read this, about which variables you are going to use. Then they need to be initialized, which means giving them an initial value. If you don't, strange things could happen. In this example, both declaration and initialization happen on the same line. Finally, we used printnumber(c).

This is the name of a function with one argument, the variable c. Assume it will take care of displaying the value: your program will only work if you also supply the code of that function, or if it was already written for you and supplied with the language as part of a library of functions.

So we have written a four line program to calculate the number 3. For such a simple task, this is at least 3 lines too many, but we needed an example.

In the variables we used, there is no mention of what type of values variables contain. In some languages, such as the C Programming Language, you have to specify what kind of variable you mean when you declare it. Following is a similar program in C:

```
int    a, b, c;
char   someletter; /* to hold a letter not a number */
char *name; /* to hold a string of letters */
float someFloat; /* to hold a floating point number */
a    = 1;
b    = 2;
c    = a + b;
printnumber (c);
```

Compiled and interpreted languages compared

The first day I used the C programming language, it was a revelation to me. I typed in my code using a full screen editor, pushed a button somewhere, and since there were no errors, I could immediately run my program to see if it did what I intended. At university, things had been different. I had to type in my `Fortran` program using a machine with punch cards, one line at a time, and leave the punch cards behind in the data center with a rubber band around it. Two days later I could pick them up together with a listing and there it was: *line 37: missing semicolon*. That was, of course, a long time ago.

Using languages that have to be compiled has advantages, although opinions may vary. By having to go through a two-step process before you can run your program, a good compiler can do a thorough job checking your code and produce all kinds of error and warning messages, like `syntax error`, `undeclared variable`, `illegal type`, and so on, including the line number and offending statement. In interpreted languages like JavaScript, and to a lesser extent maybe **PHP**, these errors are often silently ignored. Adding one line with an innocent typo into a perfectly working program can bring it to a complete stop.

Interpreted languages give you instant gratification. You type them in, using your favorite editor, as I do with `Textastic` on my iPad, immediately pull up the built in browser, and see the result (or nothing at all). You also do not have the inconvenience that you need to have a compiler present on the system when you create your programs, before you can run them. That compiler is usually part of a complete development environment.

So we set the stage for programming and learned, or relearned, a lot of important terms when it comes to programming. These are:

- Variables
- Values
- Types
- Keywords or reserved words
- Operators
- Control flow
- Functions
- Compilers and interpreters
- Libraries

- Expressions
- Syntax

Now we are going to teach you what those are: for the JavaScript language, in this chapter, and for PHP in the next chapter. Before we do that, now that we understand those words, we need to address one important topic first.

JavaScript is not the same as Java

I have already mentioned a few times about the six month class I took years ago on Web Development. Three months into it, one co-student was still mixing up Java and JavaScript. He is now a front-end developer so he must have seen the light eventually.

We want you to see it in the next *three* minutes. Java and JavaScript are both programming languages. What they have in common are the first four letters of their name, Java, which is the name of a country, and makes many people think of coffee, and some of the late Sun Microsystems. That company, together with Netscape, coined the name JavaScript, and was also the creator and promoter of the Java programming language. Therefore, it is not surprising that people are sometimes confused.

Java

Java is a programming language, developed by James Gosling of Sun Microsystems. A lot of its syntax comes from the C programming language, with some parts left out, like pointers, which happens to be my favorite part of C.

Unlike C, which is more of a "Write once, compile everywhere" language, Java is what I call a "Compile once, run everywhere" language. A Java compiler transforms a Java source code from text file to a platform independent bytecode file, so you can run it anywhere you have a Java runtime. Ever seen those messages that say you need to install a more up to date Java runtime? That is Java, not JavaScript.

Java applications typically run on server or desktop computers, but you can also use Java in Web Development. The server-side code for Web Applications, for which we will first use PHP (*Chapter 5, PHP*) in this book, could be written in Java.

JavaScript

JavaScript is a totally different programming language. Although there are "other" usages of the language, for instance using JavaScript code to modify a PDF file, we will concentrate in this chapter on what is called client-side JavaScript.

JavaScript code is interpreted and the interpreter is the web browser. The language is sometimes referred to as a scripting language. Because of the word scripting, many believed that JavaScript would be rather simplistic in nature. This is not at all true. It can be very complex. That explains why there is a second chapter in this book where we talk about JavaScript. In this one we will just stick to the things you need for classic web development.

Client-side JavaScript combines the ability of the interpreter inside the browser with the already briefly mentioned **Document Object Model (DOM)**, defined by that same browser. By being able to walk through or traverse the DOM using JavaScript code, you will be able to find the things you look for in your document and, if you would like to, modify both the content (HTML) and layout (CSS) of your document. You can also add life to your page by writing **event handlers**. These are watchdog-like functions that wait and wait until a certain event occurs, for instance a user clicking a button. Then the appropriate code is executed and our watchdog waits some more. So with JavaScript, you can program your webpages and add life to it.

Those of you who are already programmers will discover an oddity or two in JavaScript that may be hard to get used to. In many languages, a statement is not executed, nor a function called, until the previous is complete. Things tend to happen in a synchronous way, first things first. In JavaScript, things can happen in an asynchronous way: where one thing already begins before the previous has completed. At first, you may find yourself checking your code over and over again, wondering why it is not doing the things you want it to do. We will teach you what to look out for and then everything will be hunky dory. So let's get started with our first JavaScript program.

Our first JavaScript program

Create a new HTML file and add the following to the `<head>` section:

```
<script type="text/javascript">
    alert("Hello, World");
</script>
```

If you run this through a browser, a popup box will show up on the screen with the text *Hello, World* in it. If you press the **OK** button, the popup box will disappear. If you try this in a different browser, the same will happen but the popup box will look completely different. The browser renders it the way it wants and there is nothing we can do about it.

We could have also put that one line of code in a file `hello.js`, in a folder `js`, and have our program instead say the following:

```
<script type="text/javascript" src="js/hello.js">
</script>
```

Let's analyze that one line of JavaScript briefly. The line itself ends with a semicolon (`;`). It starts with `alert`, which is the name of a function that comes with JavaScript. The text for the popup is supplied as the only argument. That argument is, in this case, a string with the text *Hello, World*. To indicate that it is a string value and not a variable, we used double quotes. Single quotes would have worked too.

Variables

In JavaScript, names of variables have to begin with a letter. A few other characters, like the `$` sign, are allowed as well, but we are not going to use them. This will help us, as early on as possible, to distinguish between JavaScript variables and PHP variables. Names are also case-sensitive, so `first` is not the same as `First`.

Of course it is alright to use very short names, like a and b, but if we want to give variables meaningful names, some best practices guides recommend to use names like `firstName`, `lastName`.

Variable declarations

Variables are declared using the `var` keyword, for example:

```
var firstName;
var lastName;
var dayOfBirth;
```

Or simply everything on one line, as shown next:

```
var firstName, lastName, dayOfBirth;
```

When variables are declared but not initialized, they have `undefined` as a value, meaning there are no variable types. To assign a value to a variable, we use the = sign. So after a proper declaration, you can assign values similar to the following:

```
firstName = "Paul";
lastName = "Wellens";
```

Of course, you can also do it all in one step, as shown next:

```
var firstName = "Paul";
var lastName = "Wellens";
```

Values of variables

As we mentioned, there are no types of variables. As a value, we can assign almost anything. Following is a brief overview. But remember, we are not a reference manual, so it is not complete.

Numbers

The most common numbers are integers. Simply use the digits that make up the number, so `myNumber = 127;` assigns the **decimal** number `127` to the variable `myNumber`. The result would be different if you add a leading **zero**. The line `myNumber = 0127;` will assign the octal number `127`, which is 1*64 + 2*8 + 7 = 87 in decimal.

Hexadecimal numbers can be used as well, by starting the number with `0x`. So `myNumber = 0x127;` will store 256 + 2*16 + 7 = 295.

Finally, we can have floating point numbers. Always use a dot, never a comma, even if you are in France or other countries where the floating point is a floating comma (*virgule flottante*, excuse my French!).

```
MyFloat = 123.456;
```

Strings

A string contains zero or more characters enclosed within single (') or double (") quotes. So the shortest possible string is the empty string. Consider the following:

```
emptyString = "";
helloWorld = "Hello, World\n";
notANumber = "345";
twoLines = "First line\nSecond line";
```

You probably recognize the \n from other languages. It is an example of an escape sequence, here representing the newline character. The "345" example is an important one. The `notANumber` variable indeed contains a string, not a number.

Converting strings to numbers

There are a few convenient functions that you can use to convert strings to numbers: `parseInt()` and `parseFloat()`. They will convert a string, or initial substring, until no more numbers are found to an integer or float number. If the string cannot be converted, the function returns **Not a Number (NaN)** . Following are some examples, where we have listed what the function returns as a comment:

```
/*
Examples using parseInt() and parseFloat()
This is a multiline comment
```

```
*/

parseInt("10 yard line");          // returns 10
parseInt("one two three");          // returns NaN
parseFloat("3.14");             // returns 3.14
parseInt("3.14");            // returns 3
parseFloat("3,14");            // returns 3
parseInt("notanumberatall");          // returns NaN
parseInt("0xff");            // returns 255 which is FF
hex

/*
parseInt() can also take a second argument specifying the base of
the number to be parsed
*/
parseInt("ff",16);              // 255, same as above
parseInt("11",2);             // returns 3, 1*2 + 1
parseInt("11", 8);              // returns 9, which is 1*8
+ 1
```

Expressions and operators

This section explains how **expressions** and **operators** work in JavaScript, with a focus on what we are going to use the language for—programming websites. So do not expect an in-depth explanation of all bitwise operators, for instance. If you do not understand what I just said, that is perfectly OK. But if you need to know what they are, you will also need another book or reference.

An expression is part of a JavaScript statement, often the part on the right-hand side of the = operator, that the JavaScript interpreter can evaluate. The result will be the value of the expression. The simplest expressions we already know: values and variables. In the following example, i + 7 is also an expression. It will evaluate as 8. It contains an operator, +, in the middle. The other parts to the left and right of it can be called **operands**.

```
var i = 1;
var j;
j = i + 7;
```

We will now go over the most essential operators. To those of you who already know C, C++, or Java, they will look very familiar.

Arithmetic operators

This is the group of operators used to calculate things.

Addition(+)

The + operator adds the values of the two operands, that is, if they are numbers, as is the case in the previous example. What if they are not numbers, will the program hang? Not at all. Remember, you are going to use JavaScript to programmatically modify web pages. Web pages, in turn, consist of HTML, which are a lot of strings. So our plus operator has just become one of the most useful tools you have. Look at the following example:

```
var hello = 'Hello, World';
var htmlString;
htmlString = '<h1>' + hello + '</h1>';
```

So, in JavaScript, the plus operator can be used to glue, or, to use a more technical term, `concatenate` strings together. We will encounter the same feature in PHP but there the operator is the dot (.). It is never too soon to get used to the difference, as you will use these a lot.

In one of the examples, we used a special case of the + operator. `counter++;` is a shorthand notation people are familiar with from languages like C, that both JavaScript and PHP support. It is a shorthand notation to simply add 1 to a variable's value. So the following two statements are identical:

```
varName = varName + 1;
varName++;
```

Subtraction (-)

Everybody who has ever used a calculator knows the minus sign. It is used to subtract numbers. While the + sign could also be used with strings, that does not make sense with subtractions (nor multiplications or divisions). There is also a shorthand notation like ++ which looks like"−".

```
varName = varName - 1;
varName−;
```

They are indeed also the same.

So far, we have used one example with more than two operands, the one line statement we used to compose an HTML string. But what happens if we do the following:

```
var result;
var a = 7, b = 5,   c = 2;
```

```
result = a - b - c;
alert (result);
```

Will it be 0, or will it be 4? It is 0 because the expression is evaluated left to right, but you can remove all doubt by using parentheses. Take a look at the following:

```
result = (a - b) - c;   // 7-5 is 2 2-2 is 0
result = a - (b - c);   // 5-2 is 3 7-3 is 4
```

Multiplication (*)

The * operator multiplies its two operands.

Division (/)

The / operator divides its first operand by its second. The result is always a floating point number so 5 / 2 evaluates as 2.5. In some languages, this would be two if both operands were integers.

Modulo (%)

The % operator is extremely useful. It returns the first operand modulo the second operand. For instance, 5%2 evaluates as 1, as the quotient of the division 5/2 as an integer is 2 and the remainder is 1. I often use it in styling when I want to do something different for even things than odd things. Using if (number%2) in your code would mean odd, because it is true if the value between the parentheses is not zero.

Relational operators

A common mistake in programming is to use things like if (a = b) to compare two things and discover that it is always true even if a is not equal to b. This is because in many languages, including JavaScript and PHP, a single equal sign is the assignment operator. To check to see if two things are equal, you need (at least) two equal signs. The expressions using the operators listed next will evaluate as true or false, and in JavaScript the corresponding values are not 1 or 0, but actually true or false. Here they are:

- Equal (==): This one we use in an expression to see if two variables contain equal values, for instance if (a == b)

- Not Equal (!=): Of course this is for the opposite: true if they are not equal, false if they are

- Less than (<)

- Less than or equal(<=)

- Greater than(>)

- Greater than or equal(>=)
- Not (!)

This converts false to true and vice versa when placed in front of an expression. This can help a lot in making your program more readable.

Of course, such expressions are not very helpful when used in isolation. They need to be part of some construct where we add control to make our program do something different if the expression evaluates as false as opposed to true.

Control flow

Control flow is the heart of programming. A control flow statement helps determine which part of the code that follows it is executed and which is not. The most commonly used control flow statement in any language is probably the `if-else` statement. We will guide you through the most useful ones in JavaScript.

We learned what an expression is. I also referred to a line of JavaScript code (ending with a semicolon) as a statement. You can group statements together by putting curly braces ({ and }) around them. Such a group of statements is called a **statement block**. It is considered best practice to use curly braces even if there is only a single statement, when used in one of the controls described next, where the word statement represents a statement block.

if

The format of an `if` statement is:

```
if (expression)
{
    statements
}
```

You can also combine `if` with `else`, as shown here:

```
if (expression) {
statements
}
else {
statements
}
```

Example:

```
if (a < b ) {
alert ("a is smaller than b" );
}
else
{
alert ("a is not smaller than b");
}
```

while

Whereas an `if` statement is your basic control statement to do something, depending on a condition or something else, the `while` statement is perfect for creating a loop. A loop is a series of statements that are repeated as long as (or `while`) a certain condition is true. It is important to make sure that your condition is not forever true, otherwise you end up with an `infinite` loop.

Following is the format:

```
while (expression)
statement
```

And next is an example:

```
var count = 0;
var seriesA = "";
while (count < 100)
{
seriesA = seriesA + 'a'; // can also be written as seriesA += 'a';
count++;                  // if you forget this one you are in trouble
}
alert (seriesA);
```

The result of this code will be a pop-up of a string that contains the letter a 100 times.

switch

I like the `switch` statement. If you have to execute different code depending on more than 2 different possible conditions, using a switch statement makes for more readable and maintainable code than multiple `if`/`else` statements. Typically, the expression that is evaluated will be a variable and then there will be several statements that are executed in `case` the value of the variable is `value1`, `value2`, `value3`, and so on.

It goes as follows:

```
switch (expression)  {

case value1:
statement
break;
case value2:
statement
break;
// etc. etc.
default:
statement    // or no statement
break;
}
```

First, the expression is evaluated. Depending on the value of the expression, the statement that belongs to the matching value is executed. If there is no match, the statement associated with default: is executed. The break; statements are important, yet not mandatory. In a switch statement, the first statement block that is executed is the one that belongs to the first match. If the break; statement is omitted, subsequent statements are executed as well and that is not usually what we want. I usually write a skeleton of a switch statement, including case: and break; first and then fill it out with real code.

Now let us look at an example and have some fun with it:

```
var plate;
plate = getPlateName();
switch (plate) {
case "first":
Who();
break;
case "second":
what();
break;
case "third":
IDontKnow();
break;
case "home":
today();
break;
default:
strike();
break;
}
```

Functions

We already used some **functions** in our examples. A function is a piece of JavaScript code that you have either written on your own or is predefined by the JavaScript implementation. A function may be passed arguments, also called **parameters**. Following is an example of our own function to calculate the square root of the number that is passed as the first and only argument:

```
function square (x)
{
var sq;
sq =  x * x;
return  sq;
}
```

square is the name of the function. It consists of all the code that is in-between the curly braces. We call it a function block. Once the function is written, it can be used over and over again. The function in this example actually returns a value as well; in this case the square root of the argument. This is done by using a return statement: return sq;. Note that there are no parentheses after the return keyword, as is the case in other programming languages. That would imply that there would be a return function! So let us use our function a few times:

```
var message, result;
result = square(3);
message = "the square of 3 is" + result;
alert(message);

function square (x)
{
var sq;
sq =  x * x;
return  sq;
}
alert("the square of 4 is " + square(4));
```

As you can see, we can use the function before and after the declaration. We can store our message in a variable first or pass it along to the alert() function directly.

Scope of variables

At this point in the chapter, where we introduce functions, it is a good time to explain a very important concept: the **scope of variables,** and the notion of **global** versus **local** variables.

If you have been practicing, I sincerely hope that you have diligently declared all your variables using the `var` keyword. But what if you forgot it somewhere? Well, in that case, you have, by mistake or not, declared a global variable. So the scope, which is the region of your JavaScript program where that variable can be used, is everywhere and we call that global.

Variables declared with the `var` keyword have a local scope. Local variables are defined only within the body of the function where they are declared. Variables that are passed as arguments to a function also have the local scope, and are defined only within the body of that function.

If you declare a local variable or use a parameter with the same name as an already existing global variable, that local variable will in fact "hide" the global variable from you while you are inside the function. But if, inside a function, you assign a value to a variable without declaring it first, you may have just overwritten a value that is needed elsewhere in the program. That is why it is important to declare all your variables in the beginning of the function. Take a few minutes to study the following example and it will all become clear.

```
// global variables
outside = "outside";
global = "global";
var same ="outside"
function   testfunction()
{
// inside function
global = "local";     // mistakenly modified global variable

var inside = "inside";    // local variable
var local;
var same = "inside";

alert(inside);  // prints inside
alert (outside);// prints outside
alert(local);    // prints "" because it was not initialized
alert (same);  // prints inside
alert(global);     // prints local because we modified it

}


// running testfunction()
testfunction();

// after running testfunction()
```

```
alert (outside);    // outside
alert(global);      // global because we had overwritten it
alert(same);        // prints outside
```

Objects

Early on in this chapter, I mentioned that variables can contain almost anything: numbers, strings, or even complete employee records. But in the examples we have seen so far, there does not seem to be a suitable container for things as complex as employee records. This is where **objects** fit in. And here we will learn how to create them.

Objects are collections of named values, and they are created using a special function called a **constructor**. There are several such functions supplied with JavaScript. There is a generic one, Object(), but there are also specific ones to create objects of a predefined structure, such as Date() or String(). The syntax is as follows:

```
employee = new Object();
```

Now we have created an empty object called employee that we can fill up with names and values, as shown below:

```
employee.firstName = "John";
employee.lastName = "Williams";
employee.profession = "conductor";
```

In the context of JavaScript objects, these names are referred to as **properties**. Properties in turn have values. Objects can also contain functions that can be used to do things with what is inside an object. Such functions are called **methods**. The String() object for instance, contains quite a number of string manipulation methods. Consulting a good reference book or online reference on JavaScript Objects can result in having to write a lot less code, because it is all there already. Following is an example of a **String** method:

```
hello = new String('Hello, World"); // Or simply hello = "Hello,
World";
Hello = hello.toUpperCase();
alert (Hello);   // This will show HELLO, WORLD in a pop-up box
```

JSON

There is another way to create objects, without the need of a constructor function.

```
employee = {};  // Creates an empty object
employee.firstName = "John"; // same as before
```

```
// or do it all at once
employee = { firstName:"John", lastName:"Williams" };
```

The right hand side matches a format for data named **JavaScript Object Notation (JSON)**. We are dedicating an entire chapter on JSON in this book, where we will convince you that it is the coolest data format to use; so more about JSON later.

DOM objects, properties, methods, and events

We walked you through the basics of JavaScript objects and will now get to the essence of client-side JavaScript—programming the DOM.

The Window object

When you are running a webpage in a browser, there are two objects available to you—**Window object** and **Document object**.

The Window object gives us access to the properties and methods that can tell us about the status of the window that is used to render the webpage. We already used one such method in every single example: `alert()`. Consider the following:

```
alert("Hello, world");
```

This is actually short for the following:

```
window.alert("Hello, world");
```

Similar useful methods for creating a dialog box are `prompt` and `confirm`. The former displays a dialog box that prompts the visitor for input; the latter displays a dialog box with a message and an **OK** and **Cancel** button. Refer to the next example:

```
var response = confirm ("Are you sure you want to do this?");
if (response == true) {
// if (response) has the same effect
doit();
} else {
donot();
}
```

The window object has some interesting properties as well. You want to know how many pixels wide the current window is? You can access that by using:

```
var windowWidth = window.innerWidth;
```

The single most important property of the window object is in turn an object - the DOM Document object.

The Document object

window.document (but you do not have to write the window part) is a property that gives you an object, which contains the entire webpage that is loaded by the browser.

write and writeln methods

In most of our examples, we used the window `alert()` method to display a popup box with some text. Useful as this may be for testing or debugging, it can be annoying because you have to click the box away before you see the next line of text. Most textbooks will use the document methods `write` and `writeln` instead. With these methods, you can write your message text straight into your document. `writeln` differs from write only in the manner that it adds a new line after each statement. Simply try the following:

```
<!DOCTYPE html >
<html>
<head>
<meta http-equiv="Content-Type" content="text/html;    charset=utf-8"
/>
</head>
<body>
<p> The following text is generated using JavaScript </p>
<script type="text/javascript">
document.write("Hello, World");
document.write("On the same line");
</script>
</body>
</html>
```

Nodes and DOM traversing

We will use document methods to walk through or traverse our document and change it. You need to think of the document as a tree with nodes. What is attached to these nodes are your HTML tags with their attributes and inner HTML text. With dedicated methods, we can look for parts of our document. A **node** or **node list** is what they return (sometimes there is only one matching tag, sometimes there are more). Then, by changing the properties of these nodes or using other methods, we can effectively change the content or layout of our document.

Three useful methods for looking up things in the document tree are:

- `getElementById` : find the node with the id specified as argument
- `getElementsByClassName` : get the node(s) with the class set to argument
- `getElementsByTagName` : get all node(s) where the HTML tag equals argument

A useful property is the `innerHTML` property, which allows you to get or set the HTML text inside an HTML tag. Using these ingredients, we can cook up the following example:

```
<!DOCTYPE html >
<html>
<head>
<meta http-equiv="Content-Type" content="text/html;
charset=utf-8" />
</head>
<body>
<h1 id="hellotext"> Hello,World</h1>
<script type="text/javascript">
var  findhello = document.getElementById('hellotext');
findhello.innerHTML = ("Hello, Beach");
</script>
</body>
</html>
```

This simple HTML document, yet another `Hello, World` example, gets modified immediately using JavaScript, and the only thing we ever see rendered by the browser is `Hello, Beach`. This is not very exciting. If, however, we let the user decide when to change the text, trigger an event, and have our code react to that event, then we effectively add action to our webpage.

Events

Events are things that happen to elements inside the DOM. They can be triggered by the browser or by the user. User controlled events can be:

- Changing an input field
- Clicking a button
- Moving a mouse over an area
- Clicking on a link

You can attach an event handler to such tags that contain the code that needs to be executed. In the next example, we do so by adding an event attribute to the element. You can achieve the same by using the document addEventListener() method.

```
<!DOCTYPE html >
<html>
<head>
<meta http-equiv="Content-Type" content="text/html;
charset=utf-8" />
<script type="text/javascript">
function goToBeach() {
var  findhello = document.getElementById('hellotext');
findhello.innerHTML = "Hello, Beach";
}
</script>
</head>
<body>
<h1 id="hellotext"> Hello,World</h1>
<input type="button" onclick="goToBeach()"
value="Beach"></input>
</body>
</html>
```

The difference between the two examples is that we have added a button with an onclick attribute, which we have given the name of a JavaScript function as value, and placed our JavaScript code inside a function of the same name. Now, not until a user clicks the **Beach** button, **Hello, World** will turn into **Hello, Beach**.

Summary

At this point, you are probably thinking, now I have arrived at the hard part and I am going to get lost soon. I have good news for you! You are not going to get lost because you have already reached the end of this chapter.

We started with a brief overview of the features of a programming language. Next, we laid out what these are for JavaScript, while explaining why we need this language and how we are going to use it: to program webpages. To achieve that, we need an easy way to access all the elements in a webpage.

Well, we already learned how to access elements of a page in the previous chapter through the use of **selectors**.

jQuery, a popular and proven JavaScript library, is what we are going to use mostly for our client-side JavaScript. It lets you use CSS-style selectors to specify the elements we want to reach, even attach events to it, so we do not have to learn something new or/and have the size of this book approach that of War and Peace. jQuery has several other advantages, which we will describe in *Chapter 7, jQuery*. That includes a cool interface to switch between the *client* and the *server*.

For that reason, we are not diving into jQuery right away. We need to understand why we also need server-side programming. We are going to learn that in the next chapter and, at the same time, learn the second programming language of this book: **PHP**.

Downloading the example code

You can download the example code files from your account at http://www.packtpub.com for all the Packt Publishing books you have purchased. If you purchased this book elsewhere, you can visit http://www.packtpub.com/support and register to have the files e-mailed directly to you.

5
PHP

In the previous chapter, we discussed client-side programming using JavaScript as the language. This chapter is all about **server-side programming** and the programming language we will learn for that purpose is PHP.

PHP was originally developed by Rasmus Lerdorf, who called it **Personal Home Pages**. Today the three letters refer to **PHP: Hypertext Preprocessor**. It is a full-featured programming language that is interpreted, not compiled (we now know what that means).

When, in that 6 month class I keep mentioning, we finally reached the PHP part, I was expecting a new and unexplored topic, a new frontier. I was prepared to, as a programmer, boldly go where no one—me in particular—had gone before. Instead, all elements were utterly familiar to me.

When I explain this experience to people, I compare it to running into a girlfriend you have not seen in 15 years and realizing you still like her. Strangely enough, something similar happened to me last year, and this time it was a girlfriend.

That familiarity with PHP involved not just the language itself, being similar to the C programming language, but, in particular, all the functions that come with the language. Many of those are the same utility functions that you find in the standard C library for UNIX systems.

Introduction to PHP

As we mentioned, PHP, like JavaScript, is a language that is interpreted. So, we need an interpreter first. With JavaScript, that was easy, the interpreter is inside any browser. With PHP, you need a separate program to interpret your code. Assume you have such a program called php on your computer (I have one on my Mac) where you can type in PHP code or supply a file with the code inside it, then we could write our first program.

Our first, not so useful, example: using your favorite editor, create a file called `first.php` and enter the following text:

```
<?php
echo "Hello, world";
?>
```

Notice the strings `<?php` and `?>`. Typically, PHP code is placed in between those strings. So both examples really contain only a single line of PHP code.

So, if you have that `php` program on your computer (don't panic if you don't, you are not going to need one), you can type `php first.php` and you will see `Hello, world` appear on your screen.

As PHP is a full-featured language, you could use it this way to create standalone programs for your projects. However, this is not why you bought this book and this is not how we are going to teach you the language.

Our first real PHP program

We are going to use PHP to create **dynamic webpages**. In simple terms, these are HTML pages with PHP code embedded in them. The PHP interpreter will take your code, interpret it, and replace it with the result of your program. The resulting modified HTML document will have no more PHP code in it; that pure HTML file will be what the browser sees. Here is a good example:

```
<!DOCTYPE html>
<html lang="en">
<head>
<meta charset="utf-8"/>
<title><?php echo "Hello, world"; ?></title>
</head>
<body>
<?php
echo '<h1>Hello, World</h1>' ;
?>
</body>
<html>
```

Once the interpreter has done its thing, the contents of this file will have transformed into the exact lines of our first example in *Chapter 2*, *HTML*, and this will be what the browser sees.

Notice that in the line with the `<title>` tag, we embedded PHP code inside the HTML tag. You can do that. The second line with PHP code in our example is part of a PHP statement block. That makes it a lot more readable.

So, how can this be useful? You are pulling my leg. We are three chapters further down the road and all you can do is tell me how to write `Hello, world` in ten different ways?

Of course PHP is going to be useful. The PHP code embedded in your HTML file could be a while loop (yes, PHP has that too) that pulls data out of a file or a database, and constructs clean HTML code using that data to generate multiple pages of HTML. All of this can be done with just a few lines of PHP code. But how do we get it to work? Well, we first need to set ourselves up with a thing or two.

PHP and web hosting

So far, everything has been done by the browser, except for loading files down from the server into the browser, which the **web server** does at the browser's request - an HTTP request to be more precise.

The file that needs to be downloaded is determined by the URL, the address of a web page the user has typed in, or the link they clicked on; in this case, `www.sitename.com/demo.html` (or `demo.php`).

Once that HTML file is loaded into the browser, everything in it is read, including `<img>`, `<script>`, and `<link>` tags with `href` and `src` attributes. The browser will come up with a list of more files it needs and turn into a little Oliver Twist by going *Please Server, can I have some more?*

Once all of that code is present, the browser knows what to do with it and renders the web page on the user's computer or tablet. The `script` and `style` tags help you to distinguish which part is plain HTML and which is CSS or JavaScript.

Now, how the hell did all these files get up there, and where is *there*? They got there, and back down, because behind the name `www.sitename.com`, there is a computer and a service called **web hosting**.

Web hosting 101

We have been holding off explaining this part because so far, we could use our examples without needing a true website. With PHP, this is going to be different, so this is the place to outline which steps you need to take if you want a website of your own that people can visit.

Domain name

The first thing you need is a name for your website. What you really need is a **domain name**. Websites cannot have any name you pick and no two websites can have the same name. So, if you want to call your plumbing company's site `joe.theplumber.com`, that is not going to happen by itself.

You want to use a web hosting company to do that for you.

Web hosting companies

Web hosting companies cannot only provide you with a domain name and the registration for it, they will also (for a fee) set you up on one of their computers that run 7 days a week, 24 hours a day - 24/7 in short. That way, everybody in the world with an internet connection can visit your website anytime.

Can't I use my own computer to set up my website? Yes, you could, but as soon as you shut it down and leave the house, nobody can visit your site, and that is not what you want.

A domain name is typically `www.` followed by a string that represents a person or a company, and then one of the available endings representing the type of organization involved, or the country where it is located. Early on, there were only a few of these endings available: `.com`, `.orig`, `.net`, `.gov`, and so on. The list is still expanding.

There are sites you can visit, for example, `dns.be` for domain names in Belgium, to see whether the domain name you picked is still available. I went with `paulpwellens.com` because `paulwellens.com` was already taken by a British rugby player. Well, I am neither British, nor a rugby player.

A few years later, after I moved back to Belgium, `paulwellens.be` became available. I registered it on my name for a year but then released it as I saw no point in having two different names, and worse, two different hosting companies. But you can have more than one domain name for a single site, if you like.

Server-side setup

Once your web hosting company has set you up, it will provide you with essential information to allow you to transfer your web page files to your website. This typically involves:

- The domain name of your website (of course)
- An FTP address (an IP address or simply the same domain name)

- A login and password

- The name of a folder, for example `public_html`

With this information, you can transfer the web pages you have developed on your computer to your own site using the FTP protocol. This means that you need to have a program on your computer or tablet that can handle that. To most UNIX-based systems (Mac OS, Linux) that comes naturally, there are cool FTP apps for tablets, and FTP clients for Windows exist as well.

FTP stands for **File Transfer Protocol**. Use or install a so-called FTP client on your computer or tablet and it will let you transfer files in between it and the host, typically one file at a time. FileZilla is something to look into if you want to transfer files in bulk. And, to continue with more good news, a lot of the cool HTML editors and other tools have FTP built in.

The folder on the server that holds the home page of your site, `public_html` in our example, is often referred to as your document root.

Additional server-side services

What we just described is exactly what you need, and nothing else, to set up a static website. If you plan to use other things, and you do, it is important that you check which additional services the web hosting company you consider offers. The minimal setup connects you to a Web Server with support for the HTTP and the FTP protocol. You also need to make sure that the following is available:

- PHP - check which version of PHP

- MySQL server - also check the version

- PHPMyAdmin - a tool to easily to manage MySQL databases

Most vendors will supply some kind of panel, CPanel being a popular one, to access and configure these services. The servers themselves typically run Linux or MacOS as the operating system, Apache as the web server, and support MySQL and PHP. In www land, this combination is often referred to as the LAMP stack. How about having a LAMP of your own?

PHP development environment

There is nothing basically wrong with the setup we just described, but it holds one major inconvenience: your website will always look like work in progress. With this environment, the only way you can test the result of your work is by uploading your changes to your website using FTP and being a visitor of your own site. There is likely going to be something wrong from time to time; even the tiniest typo can do a great deal of damage.

For that reason, you want a local development environment on your computer. This allows you to only update your website periodically, when milestones of stable, tested code have arrived. In the meantime, you can develop new features, experiment, learn new things, and all of that good stuff.

To be able to develop your PHP application and test it locally you need:

- A computer running MacOS, Linux, or Windows (at the time of writing, there was not a viable PHP environment on a tablet)
- An Apache web server with PHP support
- A good code editor, a full blown **Integrated Development Environment (IDE)**, or something in between

I personally like Adobe Dreamweaver. It does everything I need and not a single thing more. It lets me look at my pages/applications and test them locally, FTP to the server with a mouse click, and its editor recognizes HTML tags, CSS properties, and JavaScript and PHP keywords. But it is not free. There are several IDEs that are free.

Either way, you should have all the files that make up your website stored in a local directory, your local document root (for example, `$HOME/Sites/mysitename`), and do your testing locally using a URL that begins with `localhost`. On a Mac, that would be `http://localhost/~username/sitename/filename.php`

Now, let's go back to the language itself. Just as we did with JavaScript, we will go through all the available ingredients in PHP that you can use to cook up a PHP program. To avoid duplication, we will not repeat what is the same in both languages, but point you to the differences. Where appropriate, we will do so in the same order.

PHP as a web development language

So, now we are ready to use PHP to write web programs, run and test them locally, and place them on a server that your web hosting company manages; in brief — to develop and deploy.

We focus on the use of PHP to generate web pages dynamically. After the PHP code is interpreted, what remains is HTML, which you should think of as strings of text that are generated on the server and rendered by the client. The data that is used to generate these pages either comes out of an external file or a database.

When invited to, the visitor of your site will interact with it. There may be a form to fill out, a button to click, a selection to be made out of several choices, and so on. The result of that intervention by the visitor needs to somehow make its way back to the server and be processed there, and all can be thought of as strings of text again. After processing, it either goes back to the client to inform the visitor and/or it needs to be stored somewhere. That somewhere is going to also be a file on the server or database.

Although I keep claiming, and I mean it, that this book is not to be used as a reference, we include a short reference on things related to strings and files, as you need them everyday. Databases are the topic of the next chapter.

Variables, values, operators, and expressions

Well, you could say that in PHP, every variable will cost you a dollar, because every variable name has to begin with a $, a dollar sign. If this little word game helps us remember the important difference between JavaScript and PHP variables, we will all save quite a few dollars over time.

```
<?php
$counter = 0;
$hello = "Hello, world";
?>
```

There is no var keyword in PHP to declare variables. You can just start using them when you initialize them. Just like in JavaScript, there are no strict types, you can use numeric and string values; PHP also uses functions, and the operators are the same unless you want to glue strings together. However, the story on the scope of variables is different.

Scope of variables

As is the case in JavaScript, the scope of a variable, the area inside a program where the variable is known and can be accessed, is a very important thing to understand. Compared to JavaScript, different keywords are used. I already mentioned that there is no var keyword. Instead, we have two new ones—global and static.

Local variables

Local variables can be accessed inside the function they are declared. It's like in JavaScript, but without the `var` keyword. Let's, once more, produce the number 3 in at least three lines:

```php
<?php
function three ()
{
$a = 1;
$b = 2;
$c = $a + $b ;
echo $c;
}
?>
```

This simply produces 3. If we were to use the variable $c outside the function in an echo statement, it would produce nothing. Yes, you heard me, nothing - not undefined, not 0, no error message, just nothing, but in a way, it is the empty string.

Here is another example. This time it does not even calculate 3:

```php
<?php
$a = 1;
$b = 2;
function nothing () {
$c = $a + $b;
echo $c;
echo $d;
}
nothing ();
?>
```

Remember the JavaScript example where we declared a variable outside a function and initialized it, and then modified its value by mistake inside a function? The declaration outside the function turned that variable into a global, without using that word in the program. Variables with the same name inside a function would hide those globals, but only if they were explicitly declared.

In PHP, we have the opposite. When we declare variables outside a function and then introduce a function in our code where we try to access them, they will simply disappear from our program horizon. So, in our example, in the statement inside the nothing() function:

```php
$c = $a + $b;
```

$a and $b are undeclared variables, and when used inside an expression, their value usually becomes the empty string. That is why nothing will appear on the screen when we use the statement:

```
echo $d;
```

The previous line however will produce the number 0. This is because it is the result of an expression containing the + operator. The operands of the expression are first converted to numeric values, so we end up adding nothing to nothing, which is the same as adding zero to zero and the result still being zero. So, how do we get access inside the function to $a and $b that we declared outside?

Global variables

It is a common practice in many programming languages to take a frequently used sequence of statements and place them together in a reusable function, for example:

```
getProductList();
```

Depending on the programming language, a function may technically not be called a function but a subroutine, a procedure, and so on. In a typical web development scenario where you need to get data out of a database, such an operation occurs frequently, so you want to organize your code that way.

Many times, I was flabbergasted because my perfectly working code stopped working once I grouped it inside a function. The reason being: my global $mysqli object that I initialized outside everything else was not reached inside my function. What appeared global to me was not treated as global by PHP. Here is the remedy:

```php
<?php
$a = 1;
$b = 2;
function nothing() {
global $a, $b;
$c = $a + $b;
echo $c;
}
nothing();
?>
```

Not until you use the global keyword inside the function will your *global* variables be treated as such.

Another remedy would be to make your $a and $b variables parameters of the function, but I would not recommend this. Using global variables declared as global inside the functions where you need them is the global best practice.

Static variables

There is a third kind of variable scope that could be very useful in some programming situations. Consider this:

```php
<?php
function listNextPrice ($price)  {
// Yes, arguments cost a dollar too
$article = 0;
$article++;
echo 'Article number ' . $article . 'costs  $' . $price  ;
//Analyze this carefully
?>
```

It is probably clear what the intent is. Each time we use this function, we want to list the price we pass as an argument, but we expect the article number to be one higher as well. However, each time we re-enter the function, the $article variable is reset to 0. Now, pay attention to this slightly different version:

```php
<?php
function listNextPrice ($price)  {
static $article = 0;
$article++;
echo 'Article number ' . $article . 'costs  $' . $price  ;
}
?>
```

This will provide the intended result because we declared $article as a static. The line with the keyword static where the variable is assigned its initial value is only used once and is ignored from that point forward when the program returns to the function. Each time it does that, however, the variable's value from the previous visit is remembered. The declaration with the static keyword cannot use an expression to initialize the variable, though.

The same selection of expressions and operators that we used in the *Chapter 4, JavaScript*, are valid in PHP, with one major, extremely important, exception.

String operators

In JavaScript, you learned that you could not only use the + sign to add numbers but also to glue strings together - concatenate them, as it is also called. In PHP, there is a separate operator to do that. It comes in two flavors, which we illustrate here:

```php
<?php
$a = "Hello";
$a =  $a   .   "World";
?>
```

Or:

```php
<?php
$a = "Hello";
$a   .=  "World";
?>
```

Most of your PHP code will be like this: concatenating strings to build up the final HTML of a dynamic page. Typically, you would start with a variable, initialize it with an opening tag, build up from there until you reach the final HTML tag, and then echo the whole lot:

```php
<?php
$htmlstring      = '<div>';
$htmlstring     .= '<h1>Hello, World </h1>';
$htmlstring     .= '</div>';
echo $htmlstring;
?>
```

Once we start adding attributes to the HTML tags, which require quotes, and start using PHP variables that contain dollar signs, it is important to pay careful attention, not only to properly use quotes, but also to which quotes to use.

To double quote or to single quote, that is the question

I am a single quote guy, I start with single quotes for every string, then switch to double quotes inside when I need them. What is the difference between them? Everything inside single quotes is taken literally, so $name reads as $name. In text between double quotes, variables are evaluated, so $name would read as whatever the value of that variable is. If you use single quotes and need variables, place them outside the quotes and use the concatenation operator to compose your text, like this:

```php
$htmlstring .= '<h2 class="blue">'.$hello.'</h2>';
```

If you want to use double quotes, the same statement has to look like this.

```php
$htmlstring .= "<h2 class=\"blue\">$hello</h2>";
```

You can leave $hello inside as it will be evaluated, but you have to escape the double quotes of the class attributes with a backslash to lift its special meaning.

My preference is to use single quotes. Just avoid mixing the two methods. On the other hand, if you have to work with code from others, make sure you pay attention to these, not always subtle, differences.

Control flow

In *Chapter 4, JavaScript*, we listed the principle control flow statements of the language: if, if/else, while, and switch. The same are available in PHP with the same syntax. Don't forget your dollars in the variable names, though!

Functions

The syntax for user-defined functions is also the same as in JavaScript.

PHP also comes with quite a few functions predefined. Some of these are so useful that we decided to include the description and syntax of them. Most of them remind me of the C library functions from my UNIX days.

String functions

As you will be using strings all the time, and will often have to manipulate those strings before the final output, it is good to know that PHP comes with a nice group of string functions. For your convenience, we include the most useful ones here.

strpos()

The strpos() function finds the position of the first occurrence of a string inside another string. It returns the position (starts at 0, not 1) or FALSE when the string is not found. The function takes two arguments: the string to look in and the string to look for:

```php
<?php
echo strpos("Hello, World","World");  // this wil print 7
?>
```

strlen()

strlen() returns the length of the string that is the only argument for this function or 0 if the string is empty.

substr()

substr() returns a substring of a string. Its typical use is substr($string,$start,$length). $string is the string used to examine, $start is the start position in that string, and the optional $length is used to specify the length of the string we want returned. The default is to the end of the string.

We can also combine these functions. What would you think the following will do?

```php
<?php
echo substr("Hello,world", strpos("Hello, world","world"));
?>
```

Date functions

It is hard to imagine a web application that never has to do anything with the time or date. Moreover, you will often have the need to use a different date format, not only because date formats differ in different parts of the world, 07/19 is correct in the US but has to be 19/07 in Europe, dates in databases use a different format as well. There are three very convenient functions to help you with that.

So, what is a date? Well it can be something that grows in warm countries and hangs on trees; I used to buy dates in Death Valley and give them to my friends. Date is also another word for an appointment, and people, young and old, can get all excited when they go on a date.

In PHP, however, the definition of date or time also comes from UNIX, and is equal to the number of seconds between now and January 1, 1970 00:00:00 GMT. Here are the three functions and how to use them.

time()

This will return the time of now in seconds. So, in the following code, you can store this in a variable:

```php
<?php
$rightnow = time();
?>
```

Please note this will be the date and time on your hosting server, which may be sitting in a different part of the world than your computer or that of the visitor of your site. You always want to specify what the correct time zone for your program is with the date_default_timezone_set function, for example:

```php
<?php
date_default_timezone_set('Europe/Brussels');
?>
```

If the date and time of your visitor needs to be determined, then that will have to happen on the client side, i.o.w. in JavaScript using its date object.

date()

The date() function is used to take a timestamp, for example, a number of seconds, or right now by default, and convert it into the format you want. The first argument it takes is a format string. Check out a good reference for a complete list of items you can use in that string. The most commonly used are m for a two digit representation of the month, d for the day, and Y for the four digit representation of the year. So, to get today's date in the European format with slashes:

```php
<?php
$eurodate = date('d/m/Y');
//or, same thing
$eurodate = date('d/m/Y', time());
?>
```

Of course, you will, from time to time, need the date and time of right now, but it is more common that you need to work with dates in the past (order dates) and the future (agenda items). So, how do we calculate the exact number of seconds between the time an order was placed and midnight of the last day in 1969? You don't. There is one more function to help us with that.

strtotime()

The strtotime() function will, in turn, return a timestamp based on the string that is passed as an argument - for instance, the format coming out of a database. Look up a good strtotime reference for a list of all valid formats. So, in practice, you will often combine the two, as in:

```php
<?php
$htmlstring .= '<td>'.date("d/m/Y", strtotime($dbdate)).'</td>';
?>
```

Arrays

An array is a collection of data elements stored in a single variable. In most programming languages that I knew before PHP, these elements would be referenced by a number, its index, starting at number 0 for the first one. What was a revelation to me, during the training I keep mentioning, is a different type of array that you can use in PHP: an associative array. More about that very soon.

Numeric arrays or indexed arrays

The traditional array with a numeric index can be declared and initialized at once, like this:

```php
<?php
$beatles    = array ("John", "Paul", "George", "Ringo" );
echo   $beatles[0].  " Lennon:;
?>
<?php
/* different way to do the same */
$beatles = array();
$beatles[]= "John';
$beatles[]= "Paul";
$beatles[]= "George";
$beatles[]="Ringo";
?>
```

In both examples, we create a 4 element array that contains the first names of the Beatles. In the first example, we do it all at once, using the `array()` constructor - similar to what we used in JavaScript to create objects. As a matter of fact, JavaScript has arrays as well, but we are not going to need them as often as we do in PHP.

The second example first tells Mr. PHP that `$beatles` is supposed to be an array, and then we start filling it up. The first `$beatles[]="John"` assignment is equivalent to:

```php
$beatles[0]  = "John";
```

The next ones will initialize the element with an index one higher. However, we could have written this:

```php
<?php
$beatles[6]  = "George";
$beatles[]  = "Ringo";
?>
```

Then George would have become the value of `$beatles[6]` and Ringo that of `$beatles[7]`. It is perfectly okay for there not to be any elements with index 2, 3, 4, and 5. People who like to collect things probably hate that. They cannot stand having 0 and 1 and 6 and 7 of something and not the ones in between. They will probably love associative arrays, just like I do.

Associative arrays

With what is called associative arrays in PHP, an index can be a string rather than a number. This is how it works:

```php
<?php
$employee = array();
$employee['first'] =  "John";
$employee['last'] = "Williams";
$employee['profession'] = "conductor";
?>
```

We have basically recreated the JavaScript object from the previous chapter as an associative array. There is also a way to initialize this all in one statement. Its syntax is new and different and introduces key/value pairs. These key/value pairs will prove very useful when we start extracting data from a database such as MySQL, because we can have MySQL return the data to us as a...guess what...associative array.

So, here is the single statement version using the special => operator:

```php
$employee = array(
"first" => "John",
"last" => "Williams",
"profession" => "conductor"
);
```

Cool control statements for associative arrays

There are more control statements than the ones we described in this and the previous chapter. The `foreach` statement is extremely useful to loop through an array, as you can easily walk through the keys and the values. The following statement loops through the array of our example:

```php
foreach ($employee as $key => $value) {
echo $key. ' is '.$value. '<br />';
}
```

Now that you've learned what associative arrays are, we are ready to explain some important array variables that we do not create ourselves, but are generated by the system: `$_POST` and `$_GET`. The most common scenario where we will have access to those is when a visitor of our site fills out a form and pushes a button.

Sending data back to the server – forms

You already know one way to obtain information from the server, and you will learn other ones when we discuss files and databases but let's first reverse it. We are going to show you how we can catch and process the information that the visitor of our site provided us with.

The most common way is when the visitor fills out fields in a form and submits it. This takes us back to *Chapter 2, HTML,* where we discussed the <form> and <input> elements. The <form> tag has more attributes than we discussed because we could not explain them at the time. In order to validate the user input, for example, to see whether a ZIP code contains only numbers before it is sent to the server, we were required to know JavaScript. We are still postponing that gig, because there is a very nice jQuery plugin to do that for us. Nor could we explain the *action* and *method* attributes, because that involved PHP. The time to do that is now.

Take a look at the following chunk of HTML, a relatively simple, partial form people can use to sign up for a newsletter.

```
<form id="myform" action="process.php" method="POST">
<label> First name </label>
<input type="text" name="first" /><br />
<label>Last name </label>
<input  type="text" name="last" /><br />
<label>Tell me about your hobbies:</label><br />
<input type="checkbox" name="hobbies[]" value="Photography">Photograp
hy</input><br />
<input type="checkbox" name="hobbies[]" value="Music">Music</input><br
/>
<input type="checkbox" name="hobbies[]" value="Theatre">Theatre</
input><br />
<input type="checkbox" name="hobbies[]" value="Tennis">Tennis</
input><br />
<button>Submit</button>
</form>
```

Imagine this code being part of a website where a visitor fills out the form and pushes the submit button. The data the user has filled in will be sent to the server and can be processed in the PHP module that is supplied with the action attribute, process.php in our example. On the other side, what has been entered as a value for the input fields will be stored in an array, named either $_POST or $_GET, depending on which method was chosen.

POST or GET, what should we get?

My personal preference is to always use **POST**, unless I need to use **GET**. So, what is the difference?

With the GET method, the data is passed along with the URL, the address of the web page you can see inside the browser. You will see things like: process.php?first= John&last=Williams&profession=conductor in the URL address bar. The string behind the question mark is called the query string.

With this method, visitors (assuming you gave them instructions) can pass along parameters that you can then process in your PHP code. It can also be useful to bookmark an interesting article that is part of large website and that you can revisit because the creator has added support for that through, for example, a query string article=number.

The two major downsides of using GET is that there is an implementation-dependent size limit (could be 1024 bytes) and that everything is visible. This is not how you want to display the login and password:

```
login.php?login=paul&password=mysecret.
```

So, in general, you want to use the POST method; there is virtually no size limit, and nothing is revealed in the URL bar of the browser:

$_POST and $_GET arrays

It is quite simple; you can find all the values that were filled out in the form in an associative array $_POST. In the case of input tags, key/value pairs are the values of the name attribute and either the value attribute or what was filled out.

We cannot be sure whether a user has filled out every required field and whether we have even done validation on the client side, which we are going to learn in a later chapter, there still needs to be validation on the server side. Otherwise, we might stuff a file or database with empty or incomplete employee records.

Note the square brackets used in the name attribute for the checkboxes. How can they all have the same name? They don't. The result of a user selecting hobbies will be an indexed array, which will be $_POST['hobbies'].

When processing your POST variables, you may want to use the isset() function. This checks to see whether the variable actually exists, which is different than checking to see whether it exists and has a value other than 0 or the empty string.

What follows is what could be code in our `process.php` module. In it, we introduce, `&&`, a logical operator. Think of it as a logical AND operator, which returns true if both what is on its left and right is true. Its counterpart is `||`, logical OR, which is true if at least one of its operands is true.

```php
<?php
if((isset($_POST['first']))) && ($_POST != "")){
$first = $_POST['first'];
}
if((isset($_POST['last'])) && (4_POST['last'] != "")) {
$last = $_POST['last'];
}
if(isset($_POST['hobbies']){
$totalhobbies = count($_POST['hobbies']);
}
?>
```

The `count()` function is a function that counts how many elements there are in an array, i.o.w. what its size is, and returns it. In our example, this would amount to the number of hobbies selected, not the number to choose from.

Files

In the previous chapters, we were dealing with inline CSS or JavaScript or, by using the correct tag and attribute, we could reference external files that contain our code. No such tags or attributes for our PHP code exist, though. But there is a different way to do that.

Let's assume that you have written a bunch of cool functions that you plan on reusing in other projects. There is no point in repeating them in between `<?php` and `?>` in every `.html` file where you want to use them. It is a far better idea to keep them in a separate file that you can reference. We have some PHP keywords to do exactly that.

include, require, and require_once

When used in a PHP statement, all three will do the same. The statement containing the keyword followed by a filename will be replaced by the contents of the file. There are nuances: if `include` is used and the file is not found, the program will continue, whereas if you use `require`, the program will stop.

The difference between `require` and `require_once` is that with `require_once`, a file that has already been loaded will not be loaded again. Make sure that you put your PHP code inside the files you include in between `<?php` and `?>` again. In the statement itself you can use parentheses or not, for example:

```
include "morecode.php"
require ("includes/functions.php");
```

Regular files

So far, we have been using all kinds of files that are stored on the server: programs (`.php` and `.js`), stylesheets (`.css`) plain web pages (`.html`), and images, used with the `<img>` tag. Those last ones can be in different kinds of format: `.png`, `.gif`, `.png`, even `.tiff`. The links in our web pages can reference even more files that reside on the server such as all kind of documents in a PDF format, or even Word. All of these files will be downloaded for the visitor of our site by the browser when needed and will have arrived on that server because we put them there, probably using FTP.

However, there are different kinds of files you could access from within your program, as well as creating or modifying new ones. After all, a well-structured file can act as a small database. There is a whole family of ready-to-use functions to handle files. Most of them take a path to a file, which is nothing else but the name itself or a number of directory names separated by a / and followed by the filename.

Those functions then return or use a file handle or file pointer. This is the part where I got *deja vu* in the training course. UNIX folks will remember that everything is treated like a file: a file proper, a printer, a hard disk, any device, and that the basic operations for files are: create, delete, open, close, read and write. For true files, text files, or binaries, there was a collection of convenient functions, all with a name beginning with an *f*. We rediscover these in PHP.

File functions or f-functions

There are functions to access existing files or create new ones, to check whether files even exist, and are actually files and not directories, and functions to read from and write to files. The first one is a little bit of a study; the rest is easy.

fopen

There is no `fcreate!`, so `fopen` is used to either create a file or open an existing one, but for what purpose? You have to carefully study the options for the second argument of this function, as that determines what happens to your file. This can go from creating a new file for writing and an existing one for reading to taking a file, destroying what is already in it and starting anew. It is also important to realize where the file pointer is pointing to. We will give you just three of these options, but they should suffice for 95% of your work. Note that we expect the value of `$filename` to be a pathname to a file.

```
$fp = fopen($filename, "r");
```

This will open the file for reading and the file pointer will point to the beginning of the file. This is typically what you want if you want to extract information from an existing file.

```
$fp = fopen($filename,"a");
```

The a stands for append. So, this will open a file for writing, starting at the end. So the end will be where the file pointer points to, and everything you write to this file will be added at the end.

```
$fp = fopen($filename, "x");
```

This is the closest to create. If the file does already exist, it will stay intact, and `fopen()` will return FALSE rather than a file pointer. Otherwise, you just created a file you can write to.

Most other options, as I mentioned, will potentially destroy the contents of your file by truncating it and you do not want that. It is like executing the command on a UNIX system - for example: `> filename`

file_exists(), is_file(), and is_dir()

To avoid surprises, you may want to check whether a file you want to open exists.

```php
<?php
if (file_exists($filename)) {
echo "$filename exists";
}
else
{
echo "$filename nowhere to be found";
}
?>
```

The file_exists() function returns TRUE if $filename exists and FALSE otherwise. It does not tell us whether it is a file or directory. For that purpose, we have the functions is_dir() and is_file().

fread and fwrite

Now, let's assume that we have files open and pointers that point to somewhere inside those files where we can read from and write to. For that purpose, we use fread and fwrite. Assume we have $fpin to read from and $fpout to write to; this would be a simple file copy piece of code, using these functions:

```php
<?php
$filecontents = fread($fpin, filesize($filename));
$success = fwrite($fpout, $filecontents);
?>
```

The second argument of fread is used to specify how many bytes you want to read. Of course, we cut it short here and said: let's read the whole file at once. For that purpose, the filesize() function comes in handy. With fwrite you can use the number of bytes you want written as an optional third argument. We did not do this in our example, we simply used the string that contains the entire file as the second argument.

One line at a time – fgets()

We used the two previous functions to read the contents of a file all in one chunk, and then wrote that chunk to another file. Many files we may use instead of a database will have lines of information organized as fixed length records that are nothing other than strings or numbers of a fixed length. Wouldn't it be nice if we could handle files line by? Well, we can. fgets() is a function that returns one line at a time:

```php
<?php
while ($line = fgets($fp)) {
/* do something with $line */
}
?>
```

The printf family

The printf function is the one that gave me that *long time no see* feeling in the, by-now notorious, six month class. It is wonderfully powerful, and if you master how to compose a good format string, you can create excellent structured output in just a few statements.

Unfortunately, you will probably discover that `printf`, the PHP version, is not going to be used a lot to produce HTML, because HTML is very far away from output of fields with a fixed length. First of all, subsequent spaces are stripped out, and by the time you see the output, the HTML tags are not shown either.

The instructor never used `printf` for two reasons - one of which is very valid. `printf` is a function, whereas `echo` is built in. So, most of the time, what you echo will be faster than what you `printf`.

So, why mention it at all? There are functions very similar to `printf` to read from or write to strings or files, and having an easy way to deal with a structured format is wickedly useful. They are: `sscanf`, `fscanf`, `sprintf`, and `fprintf`. What they all have in common is the use of a format string. First, we show you the syntax; next, we explain the format string itself.

Syntax of printf family of functions

- `printf($format, $arg1, $arg2, ... );`
- `sprintf($string,$format,$arg1,$arg2, ...);`
- `sscanf($string, $format, $arg1, $arg2, ...);`
- `fprintf($fp, $format, $arg1, $arg2, ...);`
- `fscanf($fp,$format, $arg1, $arg2, ...);`

In this syntax, `$fp` represents a file pointer that was previously created using `fopen()` and a `$string` variable to contain a string; `$arg1`, `$arg2` and so on, are variables to store the data that we retrieve, or hold the data that we want to use. `$format` holds the magic on how it is all going to be formatted:

```
<?php
$product ="Stereo receiver";
$price = 499;
printf("Item purchased: %20s - Price:%7.2\n", $product, $price);
?>
```

This will output:

```
Item purchased: Stereo receiver      - Price:0000499.00
```

This makes the product name exactly 20 characters, the price 7 digits before, and 2 after the floating point. I know, that when displayed in a browser, these extra spaces will be reduced to just one, but if `fprintf` was used to write this to a file, and we repeat the same statement in a loop, we would end up with a file with all the lines nicely lined up. It is all contained by the strings with a % sign. Typically, you have one extra argument for every % string used. Here is a selection of what they can contain:

Format values	Description
%%	What if you need a % sign—use two, only one will be shown
%b	Shows the value as a binary number, that is, only zeroes and ones
%c	The character according to the ASCII value
%d	Shows the value as a decimal number
%f	Floating-point number
%o	Octal number
%x	Hexadecimal number (lowercase letters)
%X	Hexadecimal number (uppercase letters)
%s	Treat the value as a string. You will use this the most, combined with additional format values, which are placed between the % and the letter (example %.2f): • [0-9] (Specifies the minimum width held of to the variable value) • [0-9] (Specifies the number of decimal digits or maximum string length)

Summary

In this chapter, we introduced the PHP programming language and what it takes to get you up and running to use it in your web pages. That was exactly the focus of this chapter - not to give you an in-depth coverage of everything that the language can do, even in the context of web development. We did not address the object-oriented aspects of the language, nor did we cover website-specific things, such as cookies and sessions.

We immediately zoomed into what everyone would need in PHP. We ended the chapter with a discussion on how to exchange data between client and server and use files to store that data. The functions allow us to add structure to these files. There can be even more structure in a file if you use a format such as XML, which is very similar to HTML. There are cool PHP libraries to deal with those, such as **SimpleXML**, which we will discuss in *Chapter 10, XML and JSON*.

Ultimately, you want to go beyond the use of files to hold your data and use a true database. The most commonly used database in the world of PHP-based web development is MySQL and that is the topic of our next chapter.

6
PHP and MySQL

In the previous chapter, we discussed PHP as a language for server-side programming. Its main use is to generate HTML dynamically to create web pages that are delivered to the client by the web server, as well as to store, retrieve, and manipulate data on the server. We have used files as the containers for that data, but we have given more than one hint that as soon as the amount of data becomes large and/or complex, we want to use a database instead.

In this final chapter of the first part of the book, we introduce MySQL, a database of choice for many who do web development. You may have heard of the LAMP stack. This is the M in **LAMP (Linux/Apache/MySQL/PHP)**.

Before diving into MySQL itself, and the way to interface with it in PHP (hence the title of this chapter), we would like to give you a casual introduction to databases in general.

Databases

A database is nothing more than a collection of data, usually organized in some structured way. We use databases everyday although we might not think of them as databases. Take a phone directory, for instance. It contains a lot of data. The data itself consists of names, addresses, and, of course, phone numbers, typically sorted by last name. This paper database has many disadvantages, though. Once it is printed, it will be incomplete and out of date. And if we want to look up the phone numbers of all the people that live in the same street, we would not know where to start. But it is a database, alright.

Relational databases

The term **relational databases** dates back to an article written in 1970 by Edgar Frank Codd, working at IBM at the time, called *A Relational Model of Data for Large Shared Data Banks.*

It presents a model that shows the relationships between the different elements of data and heavily uses tables. In each of those tables, there are several fields or columns that can contain data of various types (strings, numbers, dates, and so on). Entries in those tables are called **rows**, and the first column in each row is an index or primary key, a number, which is usually not changed after it has been created.

So there can be a table containing customer information. The index represents the customer ID, and all the other columns or fields are classical things, such as first name, last name, address, and so on. You can easily create other tables and choose what they can contain. Let's assume that we are going to sell books. We could have a table with book information, starting with a book ID, book title, author, category (fiction or non-fiction, or more categories), ISBN number, price, whether it is hardcover, softcover, or an eBook, and so on.

You could have a separate table for categories; one for authors too, and then, of course, a table for your order information. If you organize your data like this and use the customer, category, and book ID in your order information, you only need to change things in one place in your database when, for example, the customer changes address. The database you are going to learn about in this chapter works as we just described.

The workflow we are proposing is a two-step process. In the first step, we design how we want our tables to look and whether they should be part of a single database or several. Next, we are going to program our application, our website if you like, to use a database and its tables instead of a flat file.

To achieve all of this, you need to learn quite a few new things. It should not come as a surprise that one of those things is yet another programming language: **SQL**.

SQL

Many people believe that SQL stands for **Standard Query Language**, but actually it doesn't - it is just plain SQL. However, it is a language, and is some kind of a standard used to perform queries on a database. It is also one of those few programming languages that have been around for many years and is not going away soon. I started working with C when people thought of it as new, but even then it was developed ten years prior.

SQL is used to query a database and can be thought of as a command-line language, that is, things that are typed in a computer console. Here is an example:

```
SELECT * FROM CRIMINALS WHERE NAME = "JONES" AND BIRTHYEAR >
"1965";
```

Here is another example:

```
SELECT  LAST, FIRST, ADDRES FROM CRIMINALS WHERE BIRTHYEAR >
"1965";
```

If this reminds you of scenes from *The Streets of San Francisco*, or any other crime series of the seventies, you are absolutely right. What they were doing on these computer screens was looking up things in a database, and that was mostly the only thing computers were used for. In our example, CRIMINALS is the name of a table and the SELECT command is used to look up all records where (hence WHERE) a certain condition is met.

There is no need to learn the complete language: with just a few commands and condition clauses, we will have enough knowledge to create programs that can do the basic operations with a database, as soon as we have created our database(s) and tables. That set of basic operations is often referred to as **CRUD (Create, Read, Update, and Delete)**. In SQL, we can handle this with just five commands: SELECT, INSERT, CREATE, UPDATE, and DELETE. To accommodate getting data to come out of two tables rather than just one, you will learn another useful SQL feature called INNER JOIN.

To avoid repetition, we will teach the basics of these commands in the MySQL section.

MySQL

You do not have to be a mechanic to drive a car, but there has to be an engine under the hood or it will not move. To run an application that uses a database, there has to be a database engine under the hood. Database servers used to be dedicated computers; chances are Karl Malden and Michael Douglas used a database server in the TV series I mentioned earlier.

Today, database servers are usually software packages. Oracle Corporation specializes in database software; Microsoft has several SQL Server products. These packages can be installed on dedicated computers to function solely as a database server, but we can also install them on the same computer that acts as a Web Server, as well as on our own development system. The package we are going to use is called **MySQL**.

MySQL is open source, which means free, database server that was created by a Swedish company acquired by Sun Microsystems, which was in turn acquired by Oracle.

If you have installed a bundle such as **XAMPP** or **WAMPSERVER** (wampserver.com) for Windows, then you already have MySQL. If not, you can download it from mysql.com. Installation is very straightforward. Afterwards, you may have to go in your computer settings to make sure that the MySQL server is fired up each time the system is started. Like UNIX systems, MySQL has the concept of users, and the most powerful is **root**. MySQL is installed without a password for root. You want to change that right away. You can do this with the mysqladmin command. For everything else, we will use a tool or program it ourselves. Here is the command to change the root password:

```
mysqladmin -u root password yourchoiceofpassword
```

phpMyAdmin

phpMyAdmin is an open source utility written in PHP to help you administer your MySQL database(s). You do not have to use it, as there are other options, but I made it part of my workflow to create users, databases, and tables, and even populate tables initially. This is the equivalent of the set of SQL statements that SQL buffs call **schema statements**.

I also use phpMyAdmin to occasionally remove or change a table row. phpMyAdmin is part of XAMPP, so if you do not use XAMPP, you will have to download it first. It should be straightforward to use once you grasp the concepts that follow. In a worst case scenario, you can grab some articles off the Web. There is even an entire book on phpMyAdmin by Packt Publishing.

Creating databases

You could do everything with a single database and just add tables for each project. However, if your projects are sufficiently distinct and rather large, it is better to create a different database for each project. phpMyAdmin lets you do that without the need for SQL commands.

Creating and managing users

We already mentioned a root password. Root is a user that can do everything. When your program accesses the database, you do not want anybody to accidentally erase any data in a database. That is why we create other users in MySQL, with just enough CRUD privileges for your database. All you want to allow is to create, read, update, and delete (which is what CRUD stands for) records in a specific database. For that purpose, you create users, give them passwords, and assign privileges. Once again, thanks to `phpMyAdmin`, you still do not have to learn SQL commands.

Creating and managing database tables

Properly planning the tables that your database will contain is essential for success. It is best to first draft things on a piece of paper. Once you are close to what you want, you can create tables for your database using `phpMyAdmin`. You give the table a name, after specifying which database it belongs to, and start listing all the columns, or fields, their names, type, and possibly their maximum length, with the index as `primary key` first.

Once you have set that up, you can even start propagating those tables with data. For a bookstore webshop application, you can use the tool to enter the information on all the books you sell; the application itself will take care of adding customer data and order data to your database. `customers` and `orders` are of course candidates for tables. With `phpMyAdmin` you will always at least create the structure of your table, but it may be your web application that fills it with data. Here are two examples of tables: **books** and **authors**.

The books table will have the following data:

```
column          type         description
======= ======= ======= ======= ======= ======= ======= =======
book_id         integer      primary key (index) for this table

title           varchar(256) title of the book

author_id       integer      reference to the author id in the
authors table

publisher_id    integer      reference to the publisher id in the
publishers table

isbn            varchar(16)  ISBN number of book

cover           integer(4)   information on hardcover, softcover,
PDF or eBook

price           float        price of the book

pages           integer      # of pages in the book

category_id     integer      id to point to categories (fiction,
non-fiction, etc.

pubdate         date         date the book was published
...             ...          ...
```

The authors table will have the following data:

```
column          type          description
=======================================================
author_id       integer       primary key for this table
aname           varchar(50)   last name of author
afirst          varchar(50)   first name of author
birthdate       date          date the author was born
deceased        date          date the author died
gender          boolean           female or male
...             ....          ...
```

So, how do we get from the application to the database? This brings us back to PHP and the **mysqli** object.

MySQLi in PHP

Although we omitted this on purpose in *Chapter 5, PHP*, PHP has features found in object-oriented programming languages. So, rather than write functions, you can instead create objects and write methods for them. This is exactly how the PHP programming interface to MySQL works: there is one dedicated object, *mysqli*, and a number of methods. With these methods, you can connect to a database, submit queries, fetch the result, and finally close the connection.

Consider that we have a web application that is an online bookstore. The name of our database is bookstore, for which we created a user bookuser, with book**4u as the password. The database itself contains at a minimum the table's books and authors.

Let's write our first PHP program using MySQL now.

Connecting to the database

First we need to connect to the database. To do so, we need to identify which database we want to connect to, on which host the database server is running, and which database user we want to use. The host will almost always be localhost. So, here is the beginning of our program:

```php
<?php
$database = "bookstore";
$user = "bookuser";
$password = 'book**4u';   // I want to make sure asterixes do not
get expanded
$host = "localhost";
$mysqli = new mysqli();      // create a mysqli object
```

```
$mysqli->connect($host, $user, $password, $database);
$mysqli->set_charset("utf8");  // Make sure we  get data back
encoded as UTF-8
?>
```

We probably want to call the statement that calls the connect method from a function so that we can add some intelligence to give the user meaningful information when, for some reason, the connection to the database fails.

The statement about the character set is extremely important. I am an I18N guy, so I will spare you the details; I will even spare you from explaining what I18N stands for. UTF-8 is a code set that covers how letters used in many different languages are translated into numbers. This line helps you confirm that data is stored the proper way in your database.

Next, when your data is retrieved and needs to be displayed on a screen it may have to be translated into another codeset. But this way, you at least know which way you are storing your own data.

Our first SQL query, really!

In plain SQL, the simplest query to get something back from a database, stored in our table books, would be:

```
SELECT * FROM books WHERE 1;
```

This is what phpMyAdmin will suggest as the default SQL query. It can even be shorter:

```
SELECT * FROM books;
```

Notice that the query ends in a semicolon and that we do not mention the name of the database. We did that when we made the connection. All SQL keywords are in uppercase. Our WHERE clause is the simplest imaginable, as it is always true. We just added it to help us in the examples. The * tells the server to get me all columns. If you only want the title and the price, you would use:

```
SELECT title, price FROM books WHERE 1;
```

Now we are going to translate this into a pair of PHP statements. Before you read on, I suggest (assuming that you have created a database and a books table and put some books in it) that you go into phpMyAdmin, select our database, click on the **SQL** tab, type in the above query, and examine the result.

Writing a MySQL query in PHP

Our first MySQL query in PHP is quite simple. We are going to turn the query into a PHP string and call the query method to get the result:

```php
<?php
$sql = 'SELECT title, price FROM books WHERE 1;';
$result = $mysqli->query($sql);
?>
```

Fetching the result

Now, if we typed in everything correctly — at first you may have mistakenly omitted one of the semicolons on either side of the closing single quote — MySQL will have returned the title and price of every single book in our table. It has done so by returning an object that we named $result, which we can apply a few methods to.

The simplest one will give us the number of rows that were found, the most powerful one being fetch_assoc(), which will create for us an associative array that we can instantly use in a while loop. So, here is how we can generate an HTML table with a list of all book titles and prices with just a few lines of code:

```php
<?php
$numbooks = $result->num_rows;
$htmlstring = '<table><thead><tr><th>Book title</th><th>Price</th></tr></thead><tbody>';
while ($row = $result->fetch_assoc())
{
$htmlstring .= '<tr><td>'.$row['title'].'</td><td>'.$row['price'].'</td></tr>';
}
$htmlstring .= '</tbody></table>';
echo $htmlstring;
?>
```

The keys of the associative array are simply the names of the columns in the table.

Obtaining data from more than one table

Let's assume we do not want the list of all books, but just those by a single author. We want all the books by John Muir, so here is the SQL:

```
SELECT title, price FROM books WHERE author_id = ??? ;
```

Wait a minute! How can we tell which `author_id` John Muir has? We cannot. Of John Muir, we know the first and last name, and these are stored in the `authors` table. So here comes the most profoundly difficult query of the entire chapter:

```
SELECT title, price FROM books b INNER JOIN authors a WHERE
b.author_id = a.author_id AND aname = "Muir" and afirst = "John";
```

Alternatively, we could also use:

```
SELECT title, price FROM books b INNER JOIN authors a WHERE
b.author_id = a.author_id AND a.aname = "Muir" and a.afirst =
"John";
```

Notice the subtle difference? We used `a` and `b` as a shorthand notation for authors and books. Because we chose our field names wisely, there are no identical names showing up in other tables. If that were the case, we would need to specify the table name followed by a dot, as we did in the second example. Otherwise, an error message complaining about ambiguity would occur.

The results of the query are all titles and prices of books where the `author_id` in the table books is the same as the `author_id` under `authors`, and in that one, it matches the ones with `aname` set to Muir and `afirst` set to John. Notice that it is possible to get results of two different John Muirs back with this query.

This is how you can obtain data out of several tables. There are nuances, such as `LEFT JOIN` and `RIGHT JOIN`, but they are beyond the scope of this book.

Adding data

We mentioned using `phpMyAdmin` to propagate our tables. Once our application is running, we need to know how to add a date using PHP code, for instance, to add an order to the system. We will provide an example that adds a book to the books table. All the strings we use can, of course, be replaced by PHP variables. The SQL command we need here is `INSERT`:

```
<?php
$insertsql = 'INSERT INTO books  (title, author_id, price) VALUES
("My new book", "3", "38");'
$mysqli->query($insertsql);
$newestbook = $mysqli->insert_id;
?>
```

This will automatically add a row to your table, create your primary key with a value one higher than all others, insert the title, `author_id`, and insert the price into that row. All other fields will get the default value you specified while building your tables with `phpMyAdmin`.

The `insert_id` function is quite handy if you want to retrieve the value of the newly created primary key. We will use this now to change the price from 38 to 39.

Updating data

Let's assume that we want to change the price of a book or add information we did not enter when we issued the `INSERT` command to add data. This is where the `UPDATE` command is used. The syntax goes like this:

```php
<?php
$updatesql =  'UPDATE  books SET price="39" WHERE
book_id='"'.$newestbook.'";';
$mysqli->query($updatesql);
?>
```

This will change the price of the book we just added from 38 to 39.

You can find a very comprehensive online manual of all the MySQL commands on `mysql.com`, `php.net`, and many other websites; just search on Google for `mysql` `UPDATE` and it will be right there. This is why we are only giving you the basics in this chapter.

Summary

In this chapter, we explained how to add a database to the overall web development picture. Our database engine of choice is MySQL, as it is open source, has a PHP programming interface, and is available on all platforms. We introduced another programming language, SQL, and then explained how this fits into the MySQL/PHP picture.

To create and manage a database, including adding initial data to your tables, we talked about using `phpMyAdmin`, a great tool that we recommend adding to your workflow.

This chapter also concludes the first part of this book, which covers what I call classical web development. We walked through all the classical components, languages in particular, that people have been using to develop websites, and simple web applications: HTML, CSS, JavaScript, PHP, and MySQL.

In the second part of the book, we will take it a step further and show you how to write shorter code, use a single web page instead of millions to get the job done, and write everything in a smarter, different way so that your site or app will look great on all devices, from desktop to tablet to smartphone.

7
jQuery

I find **jQuery** to be one of the coolest things in web development. I was doing some self study, following the hours of the class I mentioned, at the wonderful university town of Leuven, which had an equally wonderful computer book store. This is where I discovered jQuery.

Every chapter that follows relies/depends on, and uses, jQuery so it is very important to know jQuery well from the get go. So, what exactly is jQuery? It is a popular JavaScript library, and the overall benefit of using it is that you can write cleaner, more compact code.

So, what is a library? Well, it can be a place with a lot of books in it. I, myself, like the one of the Plantijn-Moretus Museum in Antwerp, where they all printed their books themselves centuries ago. Rubens was the illustrator and house portraitist. UNIX and Java folks think of libraries as already compiled code, typically containing predefined functions, which are placed in a file of a special format and can be loaded with the program itself. JavaScript libraries also can contain predefined functions, but, other than that, they just contain readable JavaScript code.

Most JavaScript libraries come in two formats, regular or minimized, typically called `name.js` and `name.min.js`. Those minimized versions have all spaces, new lines, and so on, stripped out to make them smaller, and thus reduce download time. To use them, you can simply include them with your program.

jQuery uses CSS style selectors, which we already know from *Chapter 3, CSS*, to access DOM elements. Besides allowing you to write JavaScript code faster and cleaner, jQuery will take care of certain things, such as workarounds for browser incompatibilities, so you no longer have to write these yourself.

Obtaining the jQuery library

You can always download jQuery from `jquery.com`. You may want to use the minimized version once you go to production. During development, I would stay with the easier to read version so that you can, from time to time, add code for debugging purposes, as long as you do not forget to remove it later on.

Where to place the jQuery library on your page?

Not everyone agrees on what the right thing to do here is. There is always a concern about the amount of time it takes to load a file. There is going to be a difference if you put the statement in the `<head>` section of your document or right before the closing `</body>` tag to load the jQuery library - for example:

```
<script src="./js/jquery/jquery.js"></script>
```

The concern is the time it takes to load the library. I sometimes place everything that is a library, in other words, something that delivers functionality without actually doing anything, in the head section of the file. This means that the functionality will be loaded before the HTML.

You will always use jQuery in conjunction with your own JavaScript file, for example, `mycode.js`. This file will contain your jQuery lines of code inside the following:

```
$(document).ready(function(){
    }
```

All the code you put there will be executed after your page is loaded. As a consequence, this file needs to be placed in your file after all the HTML that makes up your page, preferably right before the closing `</body>` tag:

```
<script type="text/javascript" src="./js/mycode.js"></script>
```

jQuery UI and jQuery Mobile

jQuery UI and **jQuery Mobile** are two additional libraries of the jQuery family. jQuery **User Interface (UI)** offers you a number of widgets that you can use in the user interface part of your site. My favorite ones are `accordion` and `datepicker`. Unlike jQuery itself, which is JavaScript only, jQuery UI also comes with a whole bunch of CSS files. This means that as soon as you use one of those widgets, they will have their own look and feel.

Not to worry, jQuery provides a cool tool called **Themeroller**. With this tool, you can generate a customized set of CSS files so that the colors and other look and feel features of the jQuery UI elements match those of your own stylesheets.

jQuery mobile is another jQuery based CSS/JavaScript extension that offers you user interface elements to create **mobile first** sites and applications. You can create web pages that will work on phones, tablets, and desktops. We will dedicate an entire chapter to mobile first, and then responsive design later in this book. For now, take away that jQuery Mobile is a framework that allows you to take advantage of the hardware and gadgets of your phone in your web app, such as having a datepicker that behaves in the same way you set your alarm on your phone, automatically dialing the phone number that is on a web page by clicking on it, and so on.

We are not going to use jQuery Mobile in this book. Instead, we will present a different CSS/JavaScript framework called **Foundation**.

Using jQuery selectors and methods

One of the things that make jQuery so easy to use is that you can use CSS style selectors to look for elements in your page. So rather than having to learn more JavaScript methods, you just use what you already know. In real code, this means instead of using the following:

```
var content = document.getElementById("content");
```

You can use:

```
var content = $('#content');
```

$ () is a shorthand notation for jQuery(). If you use jQuery together with a similar library, such as Dojo, check the documentation on how to keep the two apart.

The above statement will create a jQuery object, which will contain zero or one DOM elements (because there can only be one element with the id content). The next statement can potentially contain a lot more elements, as many as there are with the class green:

```
var greens = $('.green');
```

As you can tell, this is the same as in CSS, # for an id, . for a class.

Now we can start using methods. What if we wanted to change all elements of the class green to be of the class yellow? For this purpose, we can use the addClass method:

```
$('green').addClass('yellow');
```

Of course, you probably want to replace green with yellow, so the class green has to be removed as well, for which you can use the removeClass method. One of the great features of jQuery methods is that you can nest them, so we can do all of these things in a single line of code:

```
$('green').removeClass('green').addClass('yellow');
```

We will now walk you through a number of very useful methods that you can use to change your web page on the fly, or to figure out what is on the page right now. Most of these are *getters* as well as *setters*. What this means is that you can get the value of an element, or, if you specify an argument, this will be used to set the value. Here we go.

html()

With this method, you can either get or set the HTML contents of an element:

```
var contenthtml = $('#content).html();
 // Get all the html code inside #content

var newcontent =
'<div><h2 class="unique">This is a header</h2><p>This is a paragraph</
p><p>This is a second paragraph</p></div>';

$('#content').html(newcontent);
```

The second set of instructions will replace the contents of #content with the preceding HTML code.

text()

Similar, but different to the previous method, this gets/sets the text inside an HTML tag:

```
var oldheader = $('h2.unique').text();   // Get only the text
inside the h2 element

$('h2.unique').text("This is the new text in the header");
 // Replace the text
```

attr()

This method lets us manipulate the value of an attribute:

```
var linkvalue = $('a.unique').attr('href'); // get the href
attribute value of an anchor tag

$('a.unique').attr('href', 'http://www.paulpwellens.com');
```

.val()

This method gets or sets the value of an element:

```
var inputvalue =  $('input.name').val();
```

show() and hide()

These are extremely useful methods to use in dynamic web pages. Very often, you want to generate HTML code for a part of the screen, and then display that code, and also do the opposite: make part of the screen disappear. The simple technique to achieve this is to prepare the content of a <div> element, insert it into the <div> element, and then make it visible. You would do this by having the following statement in your custom JavaScript file:

```
$('#content').show();

$('#content').hide();
```

These methods are also very useful to prevent a phenomenon known as **Flickering Of Unprocessed Content (FOUC)**. What do we mean by this? Remember the discussion about where to place your jQuery library and custom JavaScript files inside the page? Let's assume you use a JavaScript plugin that creates a slideshow by manipulating an unordered list (<ul>) of images (<img>). So, your original HTML may look like this:

```
<div id="slideshow">
<ul>
   <li>
   <img src="photos/mono.png" alt="Mono Lake">
   </li>
   <li>
   <img src="photos/monumentvalley.png" alt="Monument Valley">
   </li>
   <li>
   <img src="photos/centraalstation.png" alt="Central Station">
   </li>
</ul>
</div>
```

The jQuery plugin you are using, for instance, the **OWL Carousel** (owlgraphic.com) will take this HTML code and turn it into a fancy slideshow. However, if the connection is rather slow, you may end up seeing all your images stacked on top of each other first, with a silly bullet in front of them, and only seconds later your slideshow appears. You can work your way around this by placing the following in your stylesheet:

```
#slideshow {
display:none;
}
```

Then, in your custom JavaScript file, after the code that builds the slideshow animation, you include:

```
$('#slideshow').show();
```

This will cause nothing to be rendered on that part of the screen until the slideshow is ready.

.find()

The .find method is extremely powerful. You can find almost anything in your page and then do things with the result. Here is an example:

```
var address = $('#record').find('p.address');
```

This will look for and find all <p> elements with the class address in the element with the ID record. Once again, you can nest or chain it with other methods. The next example looks for an element with the attribute name set to id and then looks up its value:

```
var id = $('#record').find('input[name="id"]').val();
```

.parent()

Using .parent() can be even more powerful. The first example looks up the <tr> element(s) of the specified <td>, and the next example goes up three levels:

```
var tablerow = $('td.name').parent().html()   ;//
obtain the html code of the parent table row

var greatgranddad = $('a.threedeep').parent().parent().parent()
;
```

.next()

The .next() method looks sideways. It returns the sibling of the element to the right of the DOM structure, or not, if the optional selector does not have a match .next() only looks for the very next, so you will need to chain it if you want more:

```
var maybe =  $('div.left').next('.middle'); // only returns
something if the element to the
//next is of class middle

var  threetotheright =
$('#thistable').find('td.first').next().next().next();
    // in a table with first last address zipcode city records
this would get us the zip
```

.css()

Using jQuery, you can also get or set the CSS values of any given element. In the first example, we retrieve the background-color; in the second example, we set the color:

```
var bgcolor = $('#content').css("background-color");
$('#color').css("color", "teal");
```

jQuery documentation

The complete jQuery documentation and description of many more cool methods and features can be found at jquery.com.

There are many jQuery books on the market, maybe too many to determine which is the one for you; this book is not one of them. We will only walk you through all the technologies you need to do web development - jQuery being an important one.

If you need to choose your first book on jQuery, I recommend the latest edition of *Learning jQuery* by Packt Publishing.

Event handlers and jQuery

Congratulations, you have reached a major milestone in the book. This page introduces a few new concepts all at once and you are going to use a lot of them daily. Let's assume that you are building a website with a menu. The menu is built using an ordered list, and here is the code for one menu item:

```
<li id="intnews"><a href="oldsite/intnews.php"
class="news">International</a></li>
```

In your custom JavaScript file, you have:

```
$("#mainmenu").on("click", "a.news", function(e){

e.preventDefault();

var nav = $(this).parent().attr("id");

updateNewsContent(nav);

});
```

Let's first discuss the .on() part. This is the jQuery way of performing **event handling**. An event occurs when the visitor of your site performs a certain action. A typical action is the click of a mouse on a button or a link. We can then catch that event and perform certain tasks inside the function that is our event handler. In the previous example, we perform them all in a function that we called updateNewsContent().

It is important to repeat that your jQuery code can only access and manipulate DOM elements after they have been loaded. So, if you dynamically create HTML after your JavaScript has been executed, they will be not manipulated by your JavaScript code.

The way the .on() method is used can only help. In the example, we attach the .on() method to the #mainmenu element; in all likelihood a <div> that is always there from the initial page loading.

The first argument of the .on() method is the event itself; in our example, the click event. The second argument is optional, but I use all the time, and it describes the selector that we want to trigger an event. This makes this event a so-called **delegated** event. We could have also written it in this way:

```
$("#mainmenu a.news").on("click", function(e){

// same code here

});
```

This makes it a so-called **direct event**. What is the difference? If an `<a>` tag with class news is dynamically added inside the `#mainmenu` div after the initial page load and it is clicked on, the delegated event will catch that, whereas the direct event will not.

This is a common surprise during the development process, noticing that what worked before, suddenly, does not appear to be doing anything. Often the remedy is to start a new event handler inside your event handler. We will provide an example in a later chapter.

Finally, there is the function itself. Notice that it can have an argument. Inside the function, you can access that event object and apply methods and access properties. You will see some examples in the next chapter.

preventDefault()

The sample HTML code contains an anchor tag (`<a>`) with a `href` attribute, basically creating a link to a PHP file `intnews.php`. Let's assume that we use an ancient browser, or a browser with JavaScript turned off. The user clicking on the `<a>` tag would cause the `intnews.php` to be opened.

With JavaScript, we have determined what we want to happen in our event handler code, so we do not want the link to occur, we just want to stay on the same page. The `preventDefault()` method will, indeed, do what its name suggests. This technique is part of what is referred to as **Progressive Enhancement**, which will be discussed in a later chapter.

$(this)

Whereas you may find from time to time **this** in sample JavaScript code, in jQuery we use `$(this)`. Inside the function, it represents the jQuery object of the matching element(s).

updateNewsContent()

We deliberately did not describe what happens inside this sample function. In this section of the program, what typically goes on is that data is retrieved from the web server using PHP and possibly a database. You have seen just a few examples using classical web development techniques, such as specifying a PHP file as the action argument in a form, which will force us to go to another page.

We will, however, use jQuery methods that will allow us to execute PHP code on the server while remaining on the same page. The underlying technique used by these methods is called **AJAX**, and that is the subject of the next chapter.

Summary

In this chapter, we started moving away from classical web development for the first time. We introduced jQuery, a powerful JavaScript library that allows us to write cleaner and more compact JavaScript code. Moreover, it is going to be easier for us to do so, as it uses CSS style selectors to specify DOM elements, rather than JavaScript methods that we would have to learn.

How to download and where to place the jQuery library was explained. We illustrated the remainder of the chapter with examples using jQuery's most useful and powerful methods. To conclude the chapter, we introduced the jQuery way of creating event handlers, possibly the most important concept to grasp at this stage of the book.

In the next chapter, we will continue to use jQuery, not to traverse the DOM and change a little bit of content here and there, but to generate entire chunks of our page on the Web server by executing PHP code that is called using jQuery methods. Then we can use the data to update parts of our page, without ever leaving it. All of this is using a technique called AJAX.

8
Ajax

To some, Ajax is the name of a Dutch soccer team out of Amsterdam. To web developers, Ajax (also **Asynchronous JavaScript And XML (AJAX)**) is the collective name for a number of web techniques used on the client side to asynchronously retrieve data from the server. I started this chapter with this heavily loaded sentence because I always like to explain an acronym when I use it.

The A (asynchronous) is almost always present, the J (JavaScript) is a sure thing, as we are talking client side, but the X (XML) is not mandatory. Usually **JSON** is used as the data format between client and server. We will discuss both XML and JSON in *Chapter 10, XML and JSON*. In our examples, we will use the already familiar HTML format instead.

Using these techniques, a website can be modified after data is retrieved in the background, and parts of the screen can be updated without having to load a brand new page. This way, our website will begin to behave more like a desktop application, so we can safely call it a web application.

Unless properly managed, Ajax has its drawbacks. As it is all implemented using JavaScript, the desired behavior will not occur if JavaScript is switched off. In 2015, this should not be a concern. There are other drawbacks, but not without solutions to address them. That we will do, without delay, in *Chapter 9, The History API–Not Forgetting Where We Are*.

XMLHttpRequest

The Ajax technologies rely on the **XMLHttpRequest (XHR)** object that can be used in JavaScript code. It is used to send HTTP or HTTPS requests to a web server and load the server response data back into the script. As is the case with many other web technologies, implementations of XMLHttpRequest differ in various browsers. Here, again, jQuery will come to the rescue. By using jQuery and the Ajax related methods it comes with, those incompatibilities do not have any cause for concern.

Ajax and jQuery

There are several methods that come with jQuery that you can use to make what we like to refer to as Ajax calls. The most complete one is, not surprisingly, called `.ajax()`. We will start with a simple one.

Many Ajax-based sites are like that—an omnipresent menu on top, some other navigation in a footer at the bottom, and a center piece with constantly changing content. We cannot stress early enough that when we use Ajax the way we describe here, and our website is called `index.php`, no matter how often the content of the center piece changes, our current web page will still be `index.php`.

So, let's assume that we have a website with a main menu on top, and some basic content in the middle, inside a `<div>` with the id `varicontent`. It does not really matter what is inside `#varicontent` on the initial load—it is typically a nice photo banner—this is the chapter that explains what goes on when we change its content and replace it with something different.

jQuery Ajax methods

We will walk you through some of the most useful jQuery methods to use Ajax, from the very simple to more complex. Imagine a corporate website of a company that organizes seminars and exhibits. The home page, and all pages for that matter, as we never leave the page, contains a menu that visitors can use to navigate and select the topic of their choice.

So, let's show some code first - just a snippet to illustrate how it is done:

```
<div id="mainmenu">
<ul class="dropdown">
<li><a class="htmla" href="oldsite/information.html"
id="information" >Information</a></li>
<li><a id="seminars" class="htmla agenda" href="oldsite/seminars.php">
Seminars</a></li>
```

```
<li><a class="htmla" id="exhibits"  href="oldsite/exhibits.
php">Exhibits</a></li>

</ul>
</div>
<div id="varicontent">
<!-- code for things on the home page, maybe a photo banner -->
</div>
```

$.load() method

We will use the `load()` method to load not an entirely new page, but exactly the HTML we need in the section of the page where we want to replace the content:

```
$("#mainmenu").on("click", "a.htmla", function(e){
e.preventDefault();
var topic = $(this).attr("id");
updateHTMLContent(topic);
});

function updateHTMLContent(topic) {
var loadfile = "./content/" + topic + ".html";

$('#varicontent').load(loadfile);
}
```

In the sample code just given, we address any menu items that we have given the class `htmla`. The intent is to replace the content of what is inside `#varicontent` with the HTML that is inside a file that resides on the server. Notice that there is a `href` attribute in the example as well. We intend not to use it, but it can be present if we want a fallback plan in case JavaScript is not supported. We will readdress that when we discuss **progressive enhancement**. In the example, we include a link to a file located in a folder called `oldsite`.

So, in the preceding code, we have an event handler for when an `<a>` tag with the class `htmla` is clicked. The first thing we do is to actually prevent users going to the link specified in the `href` tag that would cause a brand new page to be loaded. The following line takes care of that:

```
e.preventDefault();
```

Instead, we are going to use the jQuery Ajax method `.load()`. We use the value of the ID of the anchor to determine what the name of the file is, and then we call the function `updateHTMLcontent()`.

Inside that function, we call `load()`, which will make the necessary Ajax calls underneath to go and fetch the contents of the file. Then, we replace #varicontent `<div>` with that content. Now, that part of the screen is updated, but we remain on the same page, and the rest of the screen is left intact.

$.post()

In the previous example, all we needed to do was to load some HTML. What if we want to execute PHP code on the server to dynamically create HTML and want to insert that inside our page? This is where the `.ajax()` method fits in, and in particular, the two special cases of `.ajax()`, `.post()`, and `.get()`.

As you may have guessed, the difference is, just as with HTML forms, the way that values are passed along to the server - whether as POST variables or as GET variables. Let's use the example of the second menu item, which contains an `<a>` tag of the class `agenda`. Like the previous example, we first prevent the browser from loading the file that is specified in the `href` attribute. This time, we grab the value of the ID of the parent:

```
$("#mainmenu").on("click", "a.agenda", function(e){
e.preventDefault();
var nav = $(this).attr("id");
updateAgendaContent(nav);

});

function updateAgendaContent(nav) {

$.post("./showagendalist.php", { nav: nav},
 function(data){

$('#varicontent').replaceWith(data);

} );
}
```

Now, we are asking the server to go and find the PHP file `showagendalist.php` on the server and pass it some values as POST variables, or just one, as in our example. The PHP code will be executed on the server and whatever it generates, we can catch inside a function. We will use this to insert inside the appropriate part of our page using the convenient JavaScript method `replaceWith()`. The default format expected back is HTML, but we can also use other formats, such as JSON and XML, which we will discuss in *Chapter 10, XML and JSON*.

Here is an example of what this PHP code could be like:

```php
<?php
$today = time();
$nav = $_POST['nav'];
switch ($nav)
{

  case "seminars":
  $sql = 'SELECT * FROM seminars;';
  break;
  .

      /* ... */
  default:
  break;
}

$mysqli = dbConnect($host, $usr, $pwd, $dbname) ;
date_default_timezone_set('Europe/Brussels');
$mysqli->set_charset("utf8");
$htmlstring = '<div id="varicontent"  ><div class="row">';

$result = $mysqli->query($sql);

while ($row= $result->fetch_assoc()
{

$htmlstring .= '<div class="agendaentry">';
$htmlstring .=  '<h5 class='title'>'.$row['title'].'</h5>';
$htmlstring .= '<div class="summary" >'.'$row['summary'].'</div>';

$htmlstring .= '<div class=" body">'.$row['body'].'</div>';
$htmlstring .= '</div>';
}

$htmlstring .= '</div>';   //row
$htmlstring .= '</div>'; //varicontent

echo $htmlstring;
?>
```

In the preceding PHP code, we look at the value of the single POST variable $POST['nav'] to determine which section of the agenda the visitor has selected from the menu. The name of that section has to somehow match a table in our database. Next, we pull out all articles from our database, assuming that there is a column for title, stored as text, and summary and body as HTML. We then generate the entire HTML for all the articles. The final statement is an echo statement of the entire HTML generated.

This is a practical example to show how Ajax works, but not practical at all in a real-life application. There are two reasons why the content inside #varicontent <div> will quickly become too large: not only do we show the entire content of each article, we also show all of them.

Rather than show the entire content of each article, we should only show the title and the summary, not the body text. Inside our generated HTML, we can have an <input> of the type hidden to carry the ID of the article, and we then turn the title into an anchor tag so that it becomes clickable. The jQuery event handler behind this anchor will trigger another Ajax call, and our #varicontent <div> that contains a list of article titles and summaries will be replaced by the complete content of single article upon clicking. But, yet again, we remain on the same page.

Even doing this is not going to be sufficient. Once the number of articles becomes large, the length of our #varicontent section is going to become unpleasantly long. To overcome this, we need to apply some kind of pagination and only show a given number of articles at a time. We will discuss a framework that has a **pagination** widget in *Chapter 13, Foundation - A Responsive CSS/JavaScript Framework*. In the following sample code , we have already taken into account an extra parameter we need, offset. The updated code to accommodate these changes follows later. We left out the switch statement in the PHP code. The only difference in the existing JavaScript code is that now UpdateAgendaContent() will take an extra argument for the offset. We only include the extra bits for the additional Ajax call.

The updated PHP is this snippet:

```php
<?php
$nav = $_POST['nav'];
if (isset($_POST['offset']))
{
$offset = $_POST['offset'];
}
else {
  $offset = 0;
}

$sql = 'SELECT * FROM seminars  LIMIT '.$offset.',10;';
```

```php
$mysqli = dbConnect($host, $usr, $pwd, $dbname) ;
date_default_timezone_set('Europe/Brussels');
$mysqli->set_charset("utf8");

$htmlstring = '<div id="varicontent"  ><div class="row">';
$result = $mysqli->query($sql);

while ($row = $result->fetch_assoc())
{

$htmlstring .= '<div class="agendaentry">';

$htmlstring .=   '<h5 class="title"><a
class="aid">'.$row['title'].'<input type="hidden" name="aid"
value="'.$row['a_id'].'"></input></a></h5>';
$htmlstring .=
'<div class="summary" >'.$row['summary'].'</div>';
$htmlstring .= '</div>'; // agendaentry
}
$htmlstring .= '</div>';   //row
$htmlstring .= '</div>'; //varicontent
echo $htmlstring;
?>
```

Additional JavaScript code:

```javascript
function updateAgendaContent(nav, offset) {

$.post("./showagendalist.php", { nav: nav, offset:offset}
 function(data){

  $('#varicontent').replaceWith(data);
  $("#varicontent").on("click", "a.aid", function(){
  var aid = $(this).parent().find('input').val();
  updateArticleContent (aid);
  });

} );
}

function updateArticleContent (aid)
{
 $.post("./showarticle.php", { aid: aid },
  function(data){
```

```
    $('#varicontent').replaceWith(data);

  } );


}
```

Note that we have now added an event handler inside the `updateAgendaContent()` function to trigger the right things happening when a visitor clicks on an article title. This is often necessary as, like in our example of the HTML tag, we want to trigger the event that did not exist on the page prior to the Ajax call.

$.ajax()

As we mentioned, the `$.post()` method (and there is a `$.get()` as well) is a special case of the `$.ajax()` method. The ones we used take fewer arguments than `.ajax()`, as some of them are predefined (not surprisingly, POST or GET), so, once again, jQuery makes things easier for us to write. To conclude this chapter, we will give you a summary on how the `.ajax()` methods can be used. Please check the full jQuery documentation for more details. It will be worth reading.

The overall syntax is:

```
$.ajax({name:value, name:value, ... })
```

These parameters specify one or more name/value pairs. Here is an overview of the most commonly used parameters and their meanings:

- **data**: This is data to be sent to the server. It is converted to a query string, if it is not already a string. It can be passed as an object, a string, or an array.
- **dataType**: This is the data type expected of the server response. It can be XML, HTML, text, JSON, or script. In our examples, we assumed HTML.
- **url**: This specifies the URL to send the request to. The default is the current page.
- **error(xhr,status,error)**: This is a function to be run if the request fails.
- **success(result,status,xhr)**: This is a function to be run when the request succeeds.
- **type**: This specifies the type of request (GET or POST).

So, the `$.post()` call in our last example is:

```
$.post("./showarticle.php", { aid: aid },
   function(data){
   $('#varicontent').replaceWith(data);

   } );
```

It could also have been written as:

```
$.ajax({

type: "POST",
url: "./showarticle.php",

succes: function(data){
   $('#varicontent').replaceWith(data);
}
data:{ aid: aid },
dataType: "html"

   } );
```

Summary

In this chapter, we introduced Ajax, a collection of web techniques to asynchronously collect data from the server. It is used to update only parts of the screen on websites and web applications, rather than loading an entirely new page each time.

Ajax techniques are based on the XMLHttpRequest object, but thanks to jQuery and its `$.ajax()` methods, you learned how to use Ajax in your applications without having to know anything about that object. We used the `$.load` and `$.post` methods in our examples to replace parts of our screen with HTML that is either stored or generated on the server.

Ajax can be used with other data formats, such as XML and JSON. It also has potential drawbacks, because now that we constantly update the page without actually leaving it, it will be perceived as different pages by the visitor of our site, particularly when they press the browser's back button.

These two topics: making the back key do what is expected of it, and using different data formats between the client and server are the subject matter of our next two chapters.

The History API – Not Forgetting Where We Are

9

In the previous chapter, we introduced Ajax, a collection of web techniques to update parts of the screen in web applications without having to create a link to a physically different page, have the browser request that new page from the server, and load it. Modern websites use this technique all over the place, as do their developers; Ajax is a common practice, a commodity almost.

The concept is, however, difficult to grasp by both the marketing people you have to work with and the visitors of your site. Doesn't it often occur that your marketing person asks you to add a page to the website and then wants to know what the URL is? It is **index.php**, honey, it always is. Visitors of your site who navigate through the menus will, when they hit the browser's back button, expect to look at the screen they just left. Instead they will be taken back to the website they were visiting before coming to yours, unless you use the techniques we are going to teach you in this chapter.

We will first describe the problem we are trying to solve; next, we will explain what the solution is in HTML5, as well as in HTML4 country.

The problem we are trying to solve

Imagine a horizontal navigation menu where the visitor clicks on a menu item, just like the example we used in the previous chapter. In a classical website, the browser takes the visitor to a different page, for example, `galleries.php`, with its URL displayed by the browser. However, an Ajax-based site will simply update a part of the screen and not do anything with the URL bar each time the visitor clicks a menu item. No matter how many items they choose, once they push the browser's *BACK* button, they will find themselves back at the previous page, which will be the previous true page, and typically, a different website, and this is not where he expects to be.

We will solve this problem by using a technique that will restore the website to its previous state, as we cannot take it to the previous page. Before we go through the details, let's discuss a thing or two about **pushing** and **popping** states.

The self-service restaurant

The best way to describe the technologies we are about to learn is to compare them with what you can find in any self-service restaurant. In such restaurants, you start by picking up a tray, and when you are done eating, you put the tray back. Now imagine a slightly different scenario. You are going to clean the tray before you put it back so that you can put it back on top of the same stack where you took it. The other difference you have to imagine is that, instead of having a multitude of trays that are all equally boring because they all look identical, every tray will have a different picture on it.

So, all these trays are part of a single stack. When you approach the stack, you can only see the picture that is on the top tray. If you add a tray to the stack, that picture will disappear as it is replaced by the one from the tray we place on top. We call that action **push**. Some old fashioned stacks have built-in springs, so you really have to push the tray down until it stays in place.

When you take a tray from the stack, the opposite will occur. The picture of the second tray becomes visible and the entire stack of trays pops up a little bit. That is why we call this action **pop** or **pop up**. Without self-service restaurants, there may have been no computer science, as this inspired many computer scientists in the field of formal grammar to create the theories of pop-up and push-down automata. I wrote my, obligatory to graduate, university paper on such a topic (no, we did not have a self-service restaurant there).

HTML5 History API and the history object

Browsers use a similar stack called the `history` stack. In JavaScript, you can access it through the `history` object, for which there are several methods available. The history object is part of the window object and is accessed through the `window.history` property. It has been around for years.

Normally, when the user navigates to a new page, the browser pushes the new URL on to its history stack and downloads and draws the new page. When the user presses the back button, the browser pops one page off its history stack and redraws the previous page.

But what if we use Ajax calls to update parts of the screen without needing to load a new page? Then, nothing is going to be pushed on to that stack by the browser. Well, that is true, unless we do it ourselves. And the key to making this possible is the `popstate` event and the `history.pushState()` function.

pushState()

Each time we create code to update part of the screen, as we did in the examples in the previous chapter, we should use the `pushState()` function to put some relevant information on to the history stack and, if we want to, change the URL string that is displayed by the browser. `pushState()` takes three arguments:

```
history.pushState(data, title, url);
```

The first argument should be some structured data, such as an array of key/value pairs that we make as meaningful as possible. The data should contain enough information to allow us to restore the page in the shape it was when we issued the `pushState()`.

The second argument is intended to be a title of sorts to show up in the dropdown list of the browser's history. At the time of writing, there was not a single browser that implemented this.

The third argument, finally, is used to pass a string that is going to be our substitute URL for this state of the page. It is displayed by the browser, so once again, the visitor will believe he has landed on a different page. That URL string has a second purpose, which we will see at the end of this chapter. So, a possible `pushState()` statement related to some of the examples could be:

```
url ="?anchor=agenda&key=" + nav;
updateAgendaContent(nav);  // this updates part of the screen
history.pushState({key:nav, anchor:"agenda"}, "", url);
```

So, the plate we just pushed on top of our stack in the browser self-service restaurant will have a picture of a key on it, labeled with the value of the variable `nav`, and a picture of an anchor, labeled `agenda`. The URL will be the same as before with a query string appended to it that also contains those two key/value pairs.

popstate event

After you've used the `history.pushState()` function to push a fake URL to the browser's `history` stack, when the user presses the back button, the browser will fire a `popstate` event on the `window` object. This is our chance to create the illusion that there are actually different pages and that we are moving our visitor back to what they believe is the previous one.

For this purpose, we create an event handler to execute some code each time a `popstate` event occurs. Most of the code we already have, because we used a function to draw a portion of the screen. We can simply reuse that.

```
window.addEventListener('popstate', function(event) {
if (event.state){
switch (event.state.anchor) {

case "agenda":
  updateAgendaContent(event.state.key);
 break;
 ..
}

}
else
{
restoreHomePage();
}
});
```

So, in the preceding code, we act on each `popstate` event by looking at our stack. If it is not empty but has a picture of an anchor labeled `agenda`, we look for the value of `key` and call the function `updateAgendaContent()`, with `key` as argument, to restore the part of the screen we always update to its previous state. Of course, this time we are not going to call `pushState()`. If we were, subsequent pushing of the back key would have no visible effect.

There is also the special case where we have run out of trays when the stack is empty. Then, we will need code that we may have not written yet. In the example, I used a placeholder function named `restoreHomePage()`. What should that function do? It should replace the variable portion of our screen with the initial content it had when our page was first loaded.

popstate and different browsers

At the time of writing, some browsers behaved differently than others. The current version of Safari will issue a `popstate` event on the initial page load, which can be utterly confusing. This also means that, in Safari, the `restoreHomePage` function will be called right after the initial page load. What that will do if your function is written correctly is replace the variable part of the screen with the exact same thing it already contains. Silly, isn't it? This may cause a small delay, and maybe some flickering, if the network is slow.

The History plugin

The popstate event and pushState method are part of the so-called **History API** that was introduced in HTML5. This means that our magic will only work if HTML5 capable browsers are used. That is, of course, not good enough. There are still a lot of people that visit your site using HTML4 capable browsers, so what do we do?

Fortunately, several plugins for jQuery exist that allow you to use the same, or a similar, API and have your code work in both types of browsers. One even has a name that will make you think of self-service restaurants again (*BBQ*), but I have been using the so-called jQuery history plugin. At the time of writing, the plugin could be found at https://github.com/browserstate/history.js.

Bookmarking

Let's move back from the self-service restaurant to our marketing person who wants to know which URL they can use to put in a document as a link to a page so that people can quickly access information that is found on the site. Perhaps they also want to know what to do if a visitor uses the bookmark feature of the browser to save the URL of a (in our case, virtual) page to revisit later. We can support this thanks to the URL parts we used in our pushState code.

In our examples, we made sure that we stored enough information about our updated page in the state that we pushed on the history stack, and you learned how to restore our page to its previous state using that information. In our pushState code, we appended a query string to the URL that basically contains the same information. We can retrieve that information using the location object of the browser and its href property. Here is the code that will, if the URL with query string is used, cause our single page website to go to the expected state:

```
$(document).ready(function(){
var url = location.href;
  if (url) {
  var urlData = url.QueryStringToJSON();
    if (urlData.anchor) {
      var anchor = urlData.anchor;
      var topic = urlData.key;
      switch (anchor) {
      case "agenda":
       updateAgendaContent(topic);
       history.pushState({key:topic, anchor:anchor},
topic, url);
```

```
        break;
      }
    }
  }
});
```

Note that we have come a long way already. A few chapters back we would have guessed this to be only possible in a huge chunk of PHP code using GET variables to get to our key/value pairs, but now this is written entirely in JavaScript and Ajax.

In the previous example, a function was used called `QueryStringToJSON()`. This is not a standard JavaScript function. It is something you can write yourself or, like I did, grab off the Web. It dissects a query string and stores the key/value pairs into a JSON object. Yes, JSON! And what JSON is all about you will learn in the next chapter.

Summary

In this chapter, we addressed one of the main drawbacks of using Ajax. You learned how to use the HTML5 History API to create the expected behavior when a visitor of our site pushes the browser's back key, or drops a URL that they previously bookmarked, into the browser's URL bar. Even though this API is for HTML5 capable browsers, you learned that there are jQuery plugins around to support this magic in HTML4 capable browsers as well.

In the last few chapters, we started using Ajax more often to update only a portion of the screen, and to remain on the same page rather than loading a new one. As a consequence, we are exchanging smaller, but more frequent chunks of data between client and server. In the examples so far, the format of our data was HTML and it was all generated on the server. In the next chapter, you will learn two new formats for data exchange: **XML** and **JSON**.

10
XML and JSON

So far, we have been using HTML everywhere. It is the format for web pages, so we have used it to create static web pages. As a consequence, HTML is the format of the data that is exchanged between the server and the client during the page load of the **.html** file.

When we create web pages dynamically, our PHP code will compose lines of HTML by the time data is sent across, which will be the true data that is exchanged, not the original content of your **.php** file. When we used Ajax, we did not specify a data format as a parameter in our jQuery Ajax methods, `.post()` or `.ajax()`, because it was implicitly understood that it would be HTML.

In this chapter, we introduce two different data formats, XML and JSON. In web development, we can use them in different ways. First, they can be an alternative to your database. For simple projects, your data can be stored in a text file, rather than in a full blown database. You could even store it as plain text.

The next, and better, level up would be to use an XML file or JSON for your data. They are plain text as well, but formatted in a special way. Data stored in that format can be easily converted to HTML, bringing us back to the previous scenario.

On the other hand, we can first send the data to the client and then process it there to create the content of our pages. We will cover both scenarios in this chapter.

XML

eXtensible Markup Language (XML) is a format that has been widely adopted to exchange information between companies, documents, and programs. It has a notation similar to HTML, using tags. As a matter of fact, HTML is a special case of XML. With HTML, tags have meanings and are meant to be interpreted by a browser. In XML, tags can mean anything or nothing at all, but the rules are stricter. Of course, if you are the creator of the XML file, we hope that the tags have some meaning to you.

You, as a web developer, may never use XML, but it is important that you know that it exists. It has been created to be a data format that is both machine readable and human readable. Humans will be able to read the content that is inside, as XML files are basically text files; computer programs can read them because they are well structured. There are several areas where the XML format is applied. We only mention a few of them here:

- **Web services**: Some people or companies give access to information from their database by providing a web service. How to create web services is beyond the scope of this book. What web services typically offer you is the ability to go to a certain web address, with a query string indicating the kind of information you are seeking. The result of visiting this (virtual) site is an output stream in the XML format, which you can then process. We will teach you how to do the processing, not the creation of the service.

- **Alternative to a database**: For simple applications, or parts thereof, using a full blown database might be overkill. As we have mentioned, you could use a plain text file or, as often occurs, a `.csv` file. It is far better to use an XML file for this, as it has more structure and it may well be the structure that the customer wants from you.

XML format

The format of an XML file is actually quite simple. It is a text file than begins with a line like this:

```
<?xml version="1.0" encoding="utf-8"?>
```

This line mentions the version of XML, and so far this is only 1.0 or 1.1. The rules are so simple that there is hardly room for changes and encoding. This is called the **XML declaration**. Everything that follows is the actual XML document, which consists of tags, or elements, a closing tag for each opening tag, and text in between them. Look at this first example:

```
<?xml version="1.0"encoding="UTF-8"?>
<!- A list of people that like California ->
<californiapeople>
  <person id="1">
    <name>Adams</name>
    <first>Ansel</first>
    <profession>photographer</profession>
    <born>San Francisco</born>
    <picture/>
  </person>
```

```
<person>
  <name>Muir</name>
  <first>John</first>
  <profession>photographer</profession>
  <born>Scotland</born>
</person>
<person>
  <name>Schwarzenegger</name>
  <first>Arnold</first>
  <profession>governator</profession>
  <born>Germany</born>
</person>
<person>
  <name>Rowell</name>
  <first>Galen</first>
  <profession>photographer</profession>
  <born>Oakland CA</born>
</person>
<person>
  <name>Wellens</name>
  <first>Paul</first>
  <profession>travel guide</profession>
  <born>Antwerp Belgium</born>
</person>
</californiapeople>
```

As you can tell, there is a closing tag for each opening tag, and one tag, `<californiapeople>` appears first and only once. This is the **root**. Tags can have tags in between them, but they must be properly nested. I have given the first person tag an **attribute** and I have also included an **empty** tag there. Just like the `<br/>` tag in HTML, `<picture/>` is a shorthand notation for `<picture></picture>`. Such an element is called **self-closing**.

Because I use XML from time to time, I have a habit of always using a closing tag in HTML files, even where it is not mandatory, for example in HTML5. Other noticeable differences are that in an XML file, white space is not truncated and names of elements are case sensitive, so `<Person>` is not the same as `<person>`.

Finally, as can be expected, there are a number of characters you cannot use inside the text of your XML file: < and &. XML is going to think it reached the beginning of an opening tag. If you need the < sign , use < instead. You should remember this from when we discussed HTML entities a few chapters ago. Other entities used in XML are &amp, which solves the chicken and egg problem, that if < means <, then using & by itself cannot be allowed either. >, ', and " can be used as well, even though >, ', and " are legal characters. If you need them as part of your text, we recommend that you use the entities instead. Oh, by the way, did you notice that the syntax for comments is also the same as in HTML? There are more similarities, and we can even style an XML file!

Displaying XML files

The first time you look at an XML file, you may not see what you expect. The best way to display an XML file is to use a browser, and the browser will treat the file as it does HTML files; therefore, you will not see the tags, only the text in between them. This is another reason why I like to use Firefox as a browser.

Firefox and Chrome display the entire XML file, including the tags. The tag names are in a different color and everything is nicely indented. Firefox will also check to see whether it is a well-formed XML file and, if it is not, produce a meaningful error message pointing you to the offending line in the file.

Sometimes Firefox displays: "This XML file does not appear to have any style information associated with it. The document tree is shown below." Well, this Firefox message suggests that there can be a stylesheet for an XML file, does it not? Could that even be a CSS file? Yes it could. Just add the following line after the XML declaration:

```
<?xml-stylesheet type="text/css" href="california.css"?>
```

Then, create a CSS file with the following content. Firefox will now display only the contents of your file, not the tags, using some funky colors. Later in this chapter, you will learn that there can be other style sheets that are not CSS files.

Due to the nature of XML, all the code examples that follow are rather long. You may want to consider going to the online pages for this book on Packt Publishing's website and picking them up there:

```
californiapeople {
  background-color: #FFDEAD;
}
name, first {
  color:teal;
  font-size:20px;
```

```
   margin-top:30px;
}
name {
margin-left:25px;
}
profession, born
{
   display:block;
   margin-left:50px;
   font-size:16px;
   font-family:Baskerville, "Times New Roman",  serif;
   color:blue;
}
```

XML editors

As XML files are text files, you can use any text editor to create and edit them. **Textastic** is a fantastic editor that only costs a few bucks, which I like using, and there is a version for MacOS, as well as iOS. **Dreamweaver** users will benefit from its feature of validating XML files for the correct syntax.

However, in the world of XML, validation can be done beyond simple syntax.

XML Schema

Imagine you are working with several customers that need to provide you with data, employee records, for example, and you request that they do so using XML as the format. You have just requested yourself a big mess! As data comes in, you realize that one customer used the element `<name>` for the last name, whereas another one decided to go with `<last>`. Not only that, they probably used a different order and mix of things.

What you should have done first was to give them a definition of how you wanted the XML file to look. Then, you could have already started to write your application that will process the data before you even received that data.

There are several conventions used to define the structure of an XML file. One is called **Document Type Definition (DTD)** and another one is **XML Schema**. The nice thing about the XML Schema format is that the file that describes the structure of your XML file is also an XML file. Teaching you about either method is beyond the scope of this book. A few examples of XML Schema files are provided however.

As a start, here is the XML Schema definition for XML files that are structured like the one in our previous example:

```
<xs:schema xmlns:xs="http://www.w3.org/2001/XMLSchema">
  <xs:element name="californiapeople">
    <xs:complexType>
      <xs:sequence>
        <xs:element name="person" maxOccurs="unbounded">
          <xs:complexType>
            <xs:sequence>
              <xs:element type="xs:string" name="name"/>
              <xs:element type="xs:string" name="first"/>
              <xs:element type="xs:string" name="profession"/>
              <xs:element type="xs:string" name="born"/>
              <xs:element type="xs:string" name="photograph"/>
            </xs:sequence>
            <xs:attribute type="xs:byte" name="id" use="optional"/>
          </xs:complexType>
        </xs:element>
      </xs:sequence>
    </xs:complexType>
  </xs:element>
</xs:schema>
```

As you can probably decipher, this is a description of all the elements that can be inside the XML file, which attributes they can have, in which order they should occur, and so on.

SimpleXML

Assume we have an XML file on the server containing data that we want to use to dynamically generate a web page, as was done previously by extracting the data from a MySQL database in a PHP program. How can this be done?

There are several ways. In this example, **SimpleXML** is used. It consists of a few PHP classes with several methods to process existing XML files, or create new ones. The following example is taken from an older version of my website, which contains many galleries of photographs. The information about the photographs was stored in an XML file, one for each gallery. Each time a photograph had to be added to the site, all that needed to be done was to add a node to the appropriate XML file.

I have abbreviated the text inside the XML file, otherwise this part of the chapter would have turned into a travel guide.

The XML file

Use your favorite editor and create `practical.xml`:

```
<?xml version="1.0" encoding="utf-8"?>
<photocollection>
<title>June Lake</title>
<overview>
The June Lake Loop begins just five miles south of Lee Vining, on
US 395, ...
</overview>
<photo>
<scaption>June Lake in the Fall</scaption>
<caption>June Lake and Carson Peak in the fall</caption>
<id>Juneinthefall-31-21</id>
<story>
Each time that unfortunate day arrives that I have to leave June
Lake ...
</story>
<thumbnail></thumbnail>
<smallimg>imagessmall/junelakefall.jpg</smallimg>
<largeimg>imagespng/junelakeinthefall.png</largeimg>
<photoshop></photoshop>
<date></date>
<camera>Nikon F6</camera>
</photo>
<photo>
<scaption>Aspen by Silver Lake</scaption>
<caption>Aspen trees by Silver Lake</caption>
<id>silverlakeaspenfall98</id>
<story>In 1998, I hit the right week of the year for fall colors.
I parked by Silver Lake ...
</story>
<smallimg>imagessmall/silverlakeaspenfall98.jpg</smallimg>
<largeimg>imagespng/silverlakeaspenfall98.png</largeimg>
<photoshop></photoshop>
<date></date>
<camera>Hasselblad</camera>
</photo>
<photo>
<scaption>Gull Lake in the Fall</scaption>
<caption>Gull Lake in the Fall - Happy fishermen !</caption>
<id>gullake-648</id>
<story>
```

```
If you take the north shore road around June Lake there is a
turnoff, ...
</story>
<smallimg>imagessmall/gulllake648.jpg</smallimg>
<largeimg>imageslarge/gulllake648.jpg</largeimg>
<photoshop></photoshop>
<date></date>
<camera>Nikon D1</camera>
</photo>
<photo>
<scaption>Silver Lake</scaption>
<caption>Silver Lake - June Lake Loop</caption>
<id>silver2</id>
<story>
Any time of the year, there can be snow in June Lake. That year
there was fresh snow ...
</story>
<smallimg>imagessmall/silver2.jpg</smallimg>
<largeimg>imagespng/silver2.png</largeimg>
<photoshop></photoshop>
<date></date>
<camera>Hasselblad</camera>
</photo>
</photocollection>
```

The XML Schema file

This is the XML Schema file `photocollection.xs`, in case you are interested what it will look like:

```
<xs:schema xmlns:xs="http://www.w3.org/2001/XMLSchema">
  <xs:element name="photocollection">
    <xs:complexType>
      <xs:sequence>
        <xs:element type="xs:string" name="title"/>
        <xs:element type="xs:string" name="overview"/>
        <xs:element name="photo" maxOccurs="unbounded"/>
          <xs:complexType>
            <xs:sequence>
              <xs:element type="xs:string" name="scaption"/>
              <xs:element type="xs:string" name="caption"/>
              <xs:element type="xs:string" name="id"/>
              <xs:element type="xs:string" name="story"/>
              <xs:element type="xs:string" name="thumbnail"/>
```

```
                <xs:element type="xs:string" name="smallimg"/>
                <xs:element type="xs:string" name="largeimg"/>
                <xs:element type="xs:string" name="photoshop"/>
                <xs:element type="xs:string" name="date"/>
                <xs:element type="xs:string" name="camera"/>
            </xs:sequence>
          </xs:complexType>
        </xs:element>
      </xs:sequence>
    </xs:complexType>
  </xs:element>
</xs:schema>
```

The CSS file

This is `practical.css`, the style sheet for the HTML that will be generated from the XML file:

```
@charset "utf-8";
body {
background-color:#FFDEAD;
margin-top:10px;
color: teal;
}
#overview h1
{
  text-align:center;
}
div.simage img
{
border:3px white solid;
align:center;
}
#mysite
{
margin:auto;
width:980px;
}
div.smallmat {

  width:300px;
  float: left;
}
div.scaption {
```

```
    padding:5px;
  }
div.story {
  width:500px;
  float: left;
}

div.storybook {
  width:850px;
  float:left;
  margin:20px;
}
```

The PHP file

This is the PHP file to generate the HTML of a small picture gallery with as many photographs as there are referenced in the XML:

```
<!DOCTYPE html>
<html xmlns="http://www.w3.org/1999/xhtml">
<head><meta http-equiv="Content-Type" content="text/html;
charset=utf-8" />
<title>June Lake Gallery</title>
<link href="styles/practical.css" rel="stylesheet" type="text/css"
media="screen"/>
</head>
<?php
$xmlfile = "practical.xml";
if (!file_exists($xmlfile)) {
    exit('Failed to open practical.xml.');
}
$xml =  simplexml_load_file($xmlfile);
?>
<body><div id="mysite"><div id="overview"><h1>
<?php
echo $xml->title;
?>
</h1><p>
<?php echo $xml->overview; ?>
</p></div><div id="gallery">
<?php
$photos = $xml->xpath("//photo");
$photocount = count($photos);
$count = 0;
```

```
while ($count < $photocount) {
$htmlstring = '<div class="storybook"><div class="smallmat"><div
class="simage"><a href="';
$htmlstring .= $photos[$count]->largeimg;
$htmlstring .= '"><img class="sphoto" src="';
$htmlstring .= $photos[$count]->smallimg;
$htmlstring .= '" title="';
$htmlstring .=  $photos[$count]->caption;
$htmlstring .= '"></img></a></div><div class="scaption">';
$htmlstring .=  $photos[$count]->scaption;
$htmlstring .= '</div></div><div class="story">';
$htmlstring .=  $photos[$count]->story;
$htmlstring .=  '</div></div>';
echo $htmlstring;
$count++;    }
?>
</div></div></body></html>
```

As the name suggests, SimpleXML is simple to use. `simplexml_load_file()` returns an object that contains the entire XML tree of the file that is passed as an argument. There is a companion method, called `simplexml_load_string()`, which takes a string that contains XML as argument. Every element inside this tree can be accessed using a simple syntax.

To access the collection of all photo nodes, the **xpath()** method was used. It supports the syntax of XPath, a query language for XML files. All you need to remember here is the meaning of `//photo`. It gives us all photo nodes back, even if they are not in the top level of the tree.

Creating XML files with SimpleXML

You can also use SimpleXML to create XML files from within a program. You start with the root element as a string, and then build up your XML file by adding nodes using the `addChild()` method, which takes one or two arguments. The first one is the name of the node, and the optional second one, its value. When you are all done, you finish it off with the `asXML()` method, which will return a string containing all the XML, or store it into a file if you give it an argument. In the example that follows, we call it `xmlfiles/new.xml`.

To conclude this section on SimpleXML, here is a tiny program that recreates our XML file, but with only one photo node, and saves it as xmlfiles/new.xml:

```php
<?php
$xml =
simplexml_load_string('<photocollection></photocollection>');
$xml->addChild("title", "June Lake");
$xml->addChild("overview", "The June Lake Loop begins just five
miles south of Lee Vining, on US 395, ...");
$photo = $xml->addChild("photo");
$photo->addChild("scaption", "June Lake in the Fall");
$photo->addChild("caption", "June Lake and Carson Peak");
$photo->addChild("story", "Each time that unfortunate day  ...");
$photo->addChild("smallimg", "imagessmall/junelakefall.jpg");
$photo->addChild("largeimg", "imagespng/junelakeinthefall.png");
$xml->asXML("xmlfiles/new.xml");
?>
```

Generating our HTML on the client side

It is not necessary to always generate the final HTML on the server and then send it to the client when we use XML or JSON as the data format and use Ajax calls. As more and more powerful devices are used to access the web and run a browser inside them, generating the HTML code might as well be done inside the client.

We could use the .post() jQuery Ajax call and execute a PHP program, with SimpleXML, to pass the entire XML file as a string and then process it. Even that part is not necessary because the jQuery Ajax methods know what XML and JSON are all about. We can simply specify the path of the XML file to the .ajax() method, and jQuery will take care of the rest. This is a great candidate to use the .get() method, as we only have to retrieve data, our XML, from the server, and not send any data to it.

The following example will generate the exact same photo gallery but it is all done with Ajax and JavaScript, no PHP code is involved. The HTML file is:

```html
<!doctype html>
<html lang="en">
<head>
<meta charset="utf-8" />
<title>June Lake Gallery</title>
<link href="styles/practical.css" rel="stylesheet" type="text/css"
media="screen"/>
```

```
</head>
<script src="./js/jquery-1.10.1.js"></script>
<body>
<div id="mysite">
</div>
</body>
</html>
<script src="./js/practical.js"></script>
```

The JavaScript file is:

```
$(document).ready (function () {
$.get( "practical.xml", function( xml ) {
var jQueryxml = $(xml);  // Turn XML object into a jQuery object
var html = '<div id="overview"><h1>' + jQueryxml.find('title').text()
+ '</h1>';
html += '<p>' + jQueryxml.find('overview').text() + '</p></div>';
html += '<div id="gallery">';
jQueryxml.find('photo').each(function(){
html += '<div class="storybook"><div class="smallmat"><div
class="simage"><a href="';
var scaption = $(this).find('scaption').text();
var caption = $(this).find('caption').text();
var largeimg = $(this).find('largeimg').text();
var smallimg = $(this).find('smallimg').text();
var story = $(this).find('story').text();
html += largeimg;
html += '"><img class="sphoto" src="';
html += smallimg;
html += '" title="';
html +=  caption;
html += '"></img></a></div><div class="scaption">';
html +=  scaption;
html += '</div></div><div class="story">';
html +=  story;
html +=  '</div></div>';
    }); //close each()
html += '</div>';
$('#mysite').html(html);
}, "xml");
});
```

XSLT

Hang on in there just a little longer. JSON is just around the corner. Only one more XML technology to add to our arsenal!

Imagine two banks that create a lot of data, as banks do. Both banks use XML, and both have crafted an XML Schema file so that the formats of the XML files are extremely well defined. Now, imagine that one bank acquires the other one and inherits all that data that is in the other XML format: this is a disaster in the making. Not to worry, XSLT to the rescue!

eXtensible Stylesheet Language Transformation (XSLT) is a language that can be used to translate an XML file into another XML file. What is required is an XSLT engine and an XSL file, which describes how the one file has to be transformed into the other. All kinds of calculations can occur in the process of transforming as it is a full blown programming language. The thickest book I have on a single web development topic is an XSLT guide.

XSL files are referred to as stylesheets. They are not CSS files, but the term stylesheet is not misplaced at all. If we take an XML file and transform it to an HTML file, then we actually created a view for the XML file that goes beyond what we can do with only a CSS file. Rather than creating an XSL file for the `california.xml` example, here is an XSL stylesheet that translates the `practical.xml` file into the exact same HTML as the SimpleXML example. If you analyze what is inside, you could dissect it into three parts: which parts of the file to apply a rule (template) to, what the rules are, and inside all that, plain HTML.

Here is an XSLT example:

```
<?xml version="1.0"?>
<xsl:stylesheet version="1.0"
  xmlns:xsl="http://www.w3.org/1999/XSL/Transform">
  <xsl:output method="html"/>
  <xsl:template match="/">
  <div id="overview">
      <xsl:apply-templates select="/photocollection"/>
  </div>
  <div id="gallery">
  <xsl:apply-templates select="/photocollection/photo"/>
   </div>
  </xsl:template>
  <xsl:template match="photocollection">
  <h1>
  <xsl:value-of select="title"/>
  </h1>
```

```
<p>
<xsl:value-of select="overview"/>
</p>
</xsl:template>
<xsl:template match="photo">
<div class="storybook">
<div class="smallmat">
  <div class="simage">
  <a>
  <xsl:attribute name="href">
  <xsl:value-of select="largeimg"/>
  </xsl:attribute>
  <img class="sphoto">
  <xsl:attribute name="src">
  <xsl:value-of select="smallimg"/>
  </xsl:attribute>
   <xsl:attribute name="title">
  <xsl:value-of select="caption"/>
  </xsl:attribute>
  </img>
  </a>
  </div>
  <div class="scaption">
  <xsl:value-of select="scaption"/>
  </div>
  </div>
  <div class="story">
  <xsl:value-of select="story"/>
  </div>
  </div>
  </xsl:template>
</xsl:stylesheet>
```

This is the PHP file to handle the transformation:

```
<!DOCTYPE html>
<html>
<head>
<meta charset="utf-8" />
<title>June Lake Gallery</title>
<link href="styles/practical.css" rel="stylesheet" type="text/css"
media="screen"/>
</head>
<body>
<div id="mysite">
```

```php
<?php
$xslt = new XSLTProcessor;
$xmlfile = "practical.xml";
$xslfile = "practical.xsl";
if (!file_exists($xmlfile)) {

    exit('Failed to open practical.xml.');
}
$xml = new DOMdocument;
$xml->load($xmlfile);
$xsl = new DOMdocument;
$xsl->load($xslfile);
$xslt->importStyleSheet($xsl);
printf("%s",$xslt->transformToXML($xml));
?>
</div>
</body>
</html>
```

JSON

JavaScript Object Notation (JSON) is the other data interchange format discussed in this chapter. Like XML, it is text-based and human readable, but it also more lightweight than its counterpart. Data sent in the JSON format will take up a lot less bandwidth when data is sent over a network connection. It is used more and more in web applications today. XML files are heavier - just notice how many pages we needed to provide some examples, and requires a parser of some sort to process the data.

JSON is derived from JavaScript, and JSON code looks a lot like JavaScript objects, but there are subtle differences. However, JavaScript can be used to process JSON data, so you would not need a separate parser, as is the case with XML. Here is the same data from the `california.xml` example, but in the JSON format:

```json
[
  {
   "name":"Adams",
    "first":"Ansel",
    "profession":"photographer",
    "born":"San Francisco"
  },
  {
   "name":"Muir",
    "first":"John",
```

```
        "profession":"naturalist",
        "born":"Scotland"
    },
    {
      "name":"Schwarzenegger",
      "first":"Arnold",
      "profession":"governator",
      "born":"Germany"

    },
    {
      "name":"Rowell",
      "first":"Galen",
      "profession":"photographer",
      "born":"Oakland CA"
    },
    {
      "name":"Wellens",
      "first":"Paul",
      "profession":"author",
      "born":"Belgium"

    }
  ]
```

Notice first of all how much easier to read this is compared to its XML counterpart. It looks like an array of JavaScript objects containing key:value pairs, and that is almost what this is. In the discussion on objects in *Chapter 4, JavaScript*, we had an example with the name of John Williams in it, and a hint to the JSON format. The key difference (*key* being a key word here) is that, in JSON, the keys also have to be surrounded by double quotes. So, in the land of JSON, `name:"Williams"` would be incorrect. Let's go over the simple structure of the JSON data format. You may want to take a piece of paper and draw a little diagram for each rule.

JSON syntax

JSON data is plain text. JSON text consists of a sequence of characters that is encoded in Unicode and that conforms to the **JSON value syntax**. So, simply said, every piece of JSON data has to be a valid JSON value. There are six tokens that have a special meaning in JSON: `[`, `{`, `]`, `}` , `:`, and `,`. There are also three name tokens that have a special meaning to JSON: `true`, `false`, and `null`. These tokens are use to compose correct JSON values.

JSON values

A JSON **value** can be an object, array, number, or string or one of true, false, or null. These are the building blocks of well-formatted JSON data.

JSON objects

A JSON **object** begins with a left curly brace and ends with a right curly brace. Inside, there will be zero or more key:value pairs, separated by commas. The key or name is a JSON string. There is a semicolon in between the key and the value. The value itself can be any valid JSON value.

JSON strings

A JSON **string** begins and ends with double quotes. Single quotes cannot be used to delimit strings. However, you could have a single quote in the middle of a string. If you need a double quote, you will have to escape it with a backslash (\ ). Other two-character escape sequences are, inevitably, \\, \/, \b, \f, \n, \r, and \t. You can also use a 4-digit Unicode code of any character by having it preceded by \u.

JSON arrays

A JSON **array** is a pair of square brackets surrounding zero or more values, separated by a comma. The example seen previously is actually a JSON array that contains four JSON objects, in turn containing four key:value pairs each.

JSON numbers

A JSON **number** is always decimal without a leading zero. There can be a minus sign in front and a . as the floating point. It may have an exponent of ten, prefixed by e or E.

JSON and PHP

If you use PHP on the server side, for example, to retrieve your data from a MySQL database, and you would like to convert the data to the JSON format, this can be done easily. Simply create a PHP array containing the data. A very convenient function, json_encode(), is available, which takes a PHP array and converts it into a string that contains JSON data (notice I did not write a JSON string). There is also a function that does the opposite and translates JSON data into a PHP array: json_decode().

Here is some sample PHP code that will convert a PHP array into a PHP string that contains the same JSON array as the one in our `californiapeople` example. If this is part of a `.php` file you access from a jQuery Ajax call, you can process it as JSON on the client side. Just make sure you specify `json` as the datatype:

```
$californiapeople =  array  (
    array
    (
    "name"=>"Adams",
    "first"=>"Ansel",
    "profession" => "photographer",
    "born" => "San Francisco"),
    array
    (
    "name"=>"Muir",
    "first"=>"John",
    "profession" => "naturalist",
    "born" => "Scotland"),
    array
    (
    "name"=>"Schwarzenegger",
    "first"=>"Arnold",
    "profession" => "governator",
    "born" => "Germany"),
    array
    (
    "name"=>"Wellens",
    "first"=>"Paul",
    "profession" => "author",
    "born" => "Belgium")
  );
echo   json_encode($californiapeople);
```

JSON with Ajax and jQuery

To conclude this chapter, we will recreate our photo gallery example that we used to demonstrate how XML can be processed on the client site to dynamically generate HTML. This time, we will use JSON as the data format. Let's start with our meaner and leaner data, which will reside on the server as `practical.json`. Note that it consists of a JSON object with a single key:value pair, with another object as the value with four key:value pairs, of which the last one is an array.

Once again, this is easier to read than its XML counterpart:

```
{
  "photocollection": {
    "title": "June Lake",
    "overview": "The June Lake Loop begins  ...",
    "photo": [
      {
        "scaption": "June Lake in the Fall",
        "caption": "June Lake and Carson Peak in the fall",
        "story": "Each time that unfortunate day  ...",
        "smallimg": "imagessmall/junelakefall.jpg",
        "largeimg": "imagespng/junelakeinthefall.png"
      },
      {
        "scaption": "Aspen by Silver Lake",
        "caption": "Aspen trees by Silver Lake",
        "story": "In 1998, I hit the right week of the ...",
        "smallimg": "imagessmall/silverlakeaspenfall98.jpg",
        "largeimg": "imagespng/silverlakeaspenfall98.png"
      },
      {
        "scaption": "Gull Lake in the Fall",
        "caption": "Gull Lake in the Fall - Happy fishermen !",
        "story": "If you take the north shore road around ...",
        "smallimg": "imagessmall/gulllake648.jpg",
        "largeimg": "imageslarge/gulllake648.jpg"
      },
      {
        "scaption": "Silver Lake",
        "caption": "Silver Lake - June Lake Loop",
        "story": "Any time of the year, there ...",
        "smallimg": "imagessmall/silver2.jpg",
        "largeimg": "imagespng/silver2.png"
      }
    ]
  }
}
```

The HTML file for this is the same as for the XML example: we only need to change what is inside the JavaScript file. Here we will use a convenient jQuery function, `.getJSON()`, another shortcut of `.ajax()`. It returns a JSON object, which we can can in turn process with regular JavaScript, making the code itself simpler:

```
$(document).ready (function () {
$.getJSON( "practical.json", function( json ) {
```

```
// For debugging:
//var jsonString = JSON.stringify(json)
//alert(jsonString);
var html = '<div id="overview"><h1>' +
json.photocollection.title + '</h1>';
html += '<p>' + json.photocollection.overview + '</p></div>';
html += '<div id="gallery">';
// Use jQuery .each() function to loop through array
$(json.photocollection.photo).each(function()
{
html += '<div class="storybook"><div class="smallmat"><div
class="simage"><a href="';
var scaption = this.scaption;
var caption = this.caption;
var largeimg = this.largeimg;
var smallimg = this.smallimg;
var story = this.story;
html += largeimg;
html += '"><img class="sphoto" src="';
html += smallimg;
html += '" title="';
html +=  caption;
html += '"></img></a></div><div class="scaption">';
html +=  scaption;
html += '</div></div><div class="story">';
html +=  story;
html +=  '</div></div>';
}
);
html += '</div>';
$('#mysite').html(html);
});
});
```

Rather than using the jQuery .each() function, we could also have used a plain JavaScript for loop:

```
for (var i in json.photocollection.photo)
{
. . .
var scaption = json.photocollection.photo[i].scaption;
. . .
}
```

Two useful JSON methods

To conclude, we will mention two JavaScript methods that are part of the JSON object, and are supported by most browsers.

To convert a JSON string into a JavaScript object, you simply pass the JSON string into the `JSON.parse()` method, like this:

```
var jsObject = JSON.parse(jsonString);
```

`JSON.stringify()` can be used to do the opposite and convert a JavaScript object into a JSON string. In our example, we could have used the following, which is handy for debugging purposes:

```
var jsonString = JSON.stringify(json)
alert(jsonString);
```

Summary

In this chapter, we introduced two data formats that are used in web development. XML is used throughout in the industry to exchange data in a format that both humans and computers can read. We can use an XML file as a small database and several XML-based technologies exist to assist us, such as XML Schema, to firmly define the structure of an XML file, and XSLT to create a stylesheet to convert an XML file into another XML file, which might well be a web page. XML files can also be processed and created in PHP using SimpleXML.

JSON is the leaner and meaner format in vogue with web developers. It requires less bandwidth than XML, which is extremely beneficial when the amount of data increases. As JSON data can be processed like JavaScript objects, no additional processing code or engine is required when JSON is used.

Now, wouldn't it be nice if our data could be stored on the server in JSON as well, so none of these conversions from one format to another are needed? Yes, it would. Can we do this? Yes, we can. Just go to the next chapter.

11
MongoDB

In this chapter, we will first compare traditional relational databases with so-called **NoSQL databases** and quickly introduce **MongoDB**, a **document database**. You will learn what it is, how to get and install it, and how to create a database to insert documents. Then, you will learn how to interface with it using PHP as the language.

Relational database management systems

In *Chapter 6, PHP and MySQL*, we introduced the MySQL database and how to interface with it using the PHP language. That was not really the language to talk to the database. We used PHP to compose query strings that are lines of code in another language, native to the database **SQL**. It is used to query the database, to extract data from it, replace it, or insert it. We mentioned that SQL is one of those very few languages that has been around for many years and is expected to stick around for many more. It is used for many different databases, open source or commercial, small or large, that we collectively call **relational database management systems (RDBMS)**.

A relational database uses tables. The columns represent the type of data stored in it, the rows the data itself. You could have a table with customer data containing fields like *name, firstname, address, zipcode, city, telephone, accountnr*, and so on. All tables contain indexes that can be used in other tables to show how they are related. The values of the indexes themselves should never change. So, if a customer changes the address, the address needs to be changed in the customer table, and only in the customer table, as in all other tables, the customer will be referenced by his or her `customer_id`. This is a good thing, but as your data becomes more complex, so will the number of tables.

My experience with this is that, as soon as a record needs to contain two things of the same kind, like when someone has two addresses, you feel you need to create another table.

Queries to access data that you need to compose the HTML of a webpage and that is spread across many tables can become quite complex, one INNER JOIN after another. Once the need arises to add a table or to add a column to an existing table, you will also have to change your code.

It is a common practice in projects that use RDBMS to first define the tables of your database, and then start writing your code. The definition of your tables is put in a schema or diagram. So, each time a table needs to be added or changed, so does your schema.

In summary, as your database grows and your data becomes more complex, a lot of overhead can be created: adding tables or columns, writing complex queries, or constantly changing the schema of your database. Wouldn't it be nice to be able to use a different kind of database, where each record contains all the information you need, and nothing else? Yes, it would.

NoSQL databases

In recent years, several new database technologies emerged that are not RDBMS. Most, if not all of them, tried to solve a particular problem (instead of wanting to be a generic solution for everybody). They are collectively called NoSQL databases. The NoSQL part can be interpreted in two ways: **NO SQL**, meaning no query language available, or **Not Only SQL**, meaning the technology supports more than just SQL. NoSQL databases have become quite popular in web development.

There are several types. The group of NoSQL databases that is of interest to us are so-called document databases. What is stored in the database are documents. A document in this context is not, let's say, a Word or PDF document, but a JSON object. Document databases provide the ability to query on any field in the document, so they are, for sure, Not Only SQL databases.

What we are doing here is the reverse of what is going on with RDBMS. Every record, or document, will contain all the information we want in it, and nothing else. If an item needs to be added to a document that was never used before, we simply add it. There is no need to change a schema or a table. If a record now needs two things of the same kind, we do things the JSON way: we use an array instead of a single object.

Surprisingly enough, those databases perform and scale very well, even with thousands of documents. The NoSQL database we have chosen for our projects, and for this book, is MongoDB. It appears to be the one that has the most features, is the most widely adopted — the *New York Times* uses it! — and scales and performs well.

MongoDB

With MongoDB, we just replace MySQL with a document database that can be a better solution for our projects and has JSON as the common denominator. MongoDB uses collections and documents. So, that makes it more suitable for, for example, an online bookstore application.

As a document in MongoDB is a JSON object, to transfer data to it from PHP is as simple as storing the data in a PHP array. No more multiple tables and inner joins required. We will explain how to get to MongoDB, create a database, and add and update documents. We will do so from within a PHP program, as well as the MongoDB shell.

Installing MongoDB

Obtaining and installing MongoDB depends on the platform you are using. Go to www.mongodb.org for the software and the documentation. This will get you basically two programs. The first one is **mongod** (known as the **MongoDB daemon**), a program that needs to be up and running all the time, just like a MySQL server would. The second one is simply called **mongo** and it is **the MongoDB shell**. It is a command interpreter that lets you create databases, collections, and documents, and modify them. I like to think of it as **phpMyAdmin** for MongoDB.

If you want to access and manipulate your MongoDB database from within a program, you will also need to download and install a driver for MongoDB for the programming language of your choice. So, for PHP, we will need a PHP driver for MongoDB. Drivers can be built from source, but there is also binary available from distributions that change all the time. So, use your favorite search engine and look for a PHP driver for MongoDB. At the time of writing, there was one at php.net/manual/en/book.mongo.php.

The MongoDB shell

Once you have all these things installed, it is time to start filling up a database with documents. In MySQL, we started by first creating all our tables, maybe initially on a piece of paper, and then for real by using phpMyAdmin. In MongoDB, we use the MongoDB shell to populate our database for the first time. However, there is no need to create tables. We simply add documents. As they say in French: *simple comme bonjour*.

In order to do so, we make the distinction between databases, collections, and documents. Every instance of MongoDB can contain one or more databases. Although you can do everything with a single database, it is recommended that you use separate databases where appropriate, for example, one for each project.

Although you could put all your documents into a database, just like that, it is better to organize them as several collections. Compared to RDBMS, documents are the equivalent of table rows, and collections are the counterpart of tables.

In the remainder of this section, we will walk you through using the MongoDB shell to do basic **Create, Read, Update, and Delete (CRUD)** operations. For more detailed and advanced operations, consult the excellent MongoDB documentation at `mongodb.org` or some of the books available on the subject.

To start the MongoDB shell, simply type `mongo` in the command line. You will see something similar to:

```
MongoDB shell version: 2.6.6
connecting to: test
>
```

You are now talking to the command interpreter, which basically reads JavaScript code. By default, mongoDB will connect to a database called `test`. The > symbol is your command prompt. Just to show that it works, let's promptly change it:

```
> prompt="mongoDB "
mongoDB
```

Creating databases, collections, and documents

We have changed our command prompt to the string mongoDB. Let's connect to a different database:

```
mongoDB  use california
```

You have now switched to a database called `california`. You think I forgot something and I am telling you I did not, I just want to keep the suspense going here. Now, let's add a document to a collection `people`. Simply type:

```
mongoDB db.people.insert( {
  "name":"Adams",
  "first":"Ansel",
  "profession":"photographer",
  "born":"San Francisco"
  });
```

Let's find out whether something really happened here. There is a method to find all the documents in a collection, unsurprisingly, called `find()`:

```
mongoDB db.people.find()

{ "_id" : ObjectId("54ad4336227ad31227c3902d"), "name" :
"Adams", "first" : "Ansel", "profession" : "photographer",
"born" : "San Francisco" }
```

Oh my goodness, we now have created a database called `california`, and in it, a collection `people`, and inside it, our first document. All of this just happens; if the database or collection does not exist yet, MongoDB will create them. Unlike in MySQL, there is no need for any SQL to create the database nor table ahead of time or to specify data types.

If you type the following two commands, you will indeed see that they now exist:

```
mongoDB show dbs
...
california
...
mongoDB show collections
...
people
...
```

There is an alternate to find, which gives a nicer output, called `findOne()`:

```
mongoDB db.people.findOne()
{
    "_id" : ObjectId("54ad4336227ad31227c3902d"),
    "name" : "Adams",
    "first" : "Ansel",
    "profession" : "photographer",
    "born" : "San Francisco"
}
```

Of course, there is only one thing to find, but as the number of documents increases, we want to be more specific, so we could say things like:

```
mongoDB db.people.findOne({"first" : "Ansel"})
```

This is beginning to look very much like a query, because it is one! You may have noticed a key named "_id" and a very long value. Let's spend a few lines on this.

_id and ObjectIds

Every document stored in MongoDB must have an "_id" key. It can be any type, but it defaults to ObjectId. In a single collection, every document must have a unique value for "_id", which ensures that every document in a collection can be uniquely identified. ObjectId use 12 bytes of storage. As stated previously, if there is no "_id" key present when a document is inserted, one will be automatically added to the inserted document.

Loading scripts

The mongoDB shell interprets JavaScript and also has built-in functions. Some things you are used to will not work, such as alert(), because it is a method of the Windows object, and that is only available when you are running in a browser.

A very useful function is load(). You can prepare all your commands ahead of time and store them in a file. Create a folder for your project, go to it, and store the following, which is very close to one of our JSON examples from the previous chapter, in a file californiapeople.js:

```
db.people.insert({
    "name":"Adams",
    "first":"Ansel",
    "profession":"photographer",
    "born":"San Francisco"

  });

db.people.insert({  "name":"Muir",
    "first":"John",
    "profession":"naturalist",
    "born":"Scotland"

  });
db.people.insert(    {
    "name":"Schwarzenegger",
    "first":"Arnold",
```

```
        "profession":"governator",
        "born":"Germany"

    });
db.people.insert( {
    "name":"Rowell",
    "first":"Galen",
    "profession":"photographer",
    "born":"Oakland CA"

    });
db.people.insert(    {
    "name":"Wellens",
    "first":"Paul",
    "profession":"author",
    "born":"Belgium"

    });
```

Then, issue the following command:

mongoDB   `load("californiapeople.js")`

This will insert five more documents into the `people` collection. To verify it, type:

mongoDB `db.people.find()`

The result will look similar to this:

```
{ "_id" : ObjectId("54ad4336227ad31227c3902d"), "name" : "Adams",
"first" : "Ansel", "profession" : "photographer", "born" : "San
Francisco" }
{ "_id" : ObjectId("54ad46f6812ce43efb530a07"), "name" : "Adams",
"first" : "Ansel", "profession" : "photographer", "born" : "San
Francisco" }
{ "_id" : ObjectId("54ad46f6812ce43efb530a08"), "name" : "Muir",
"first" : "John", "profession" : "naturalist", "born" : "Scotland" }
{ "_id" : ObjectId("54ad46f6812ce43efb530a09"), "name" :
"Schwarzenegger", "first" : "Arnold", "profession" : "governator",
"born" : "Germany" }
{ "_id" : ObjectId("54ad46f6812ce43efb530a0a"), "name" : "Rowell",
"first" : "Galen", "profession" : "photographer", "born" : "Oakland
CA" }
{ "_id" : ObjectId("54ad46f6812ce43efb530a0b"), "name" : "Wellens",
"first" : "Paul", "profession" : "author", "born" : "Belgium" }
```

Removing documents

Notice that there are now two documents containing `Ansel Adams`, clearly distinct by its "`_id`". But, we only need one, so it is time to remove one. This is done using the `remove()` function. Beware, if you do not specify an argument in the following command, all documents in the collection would be removed and once documents are removed, they cannot be restored:

```
mongoDB db.people.remove( { "_id" :
ObjectId("54ad46f6812ce43efb530a07" )} )
```

Updating documents

Our final CRUD operation is update. In this example, we add a key:value pair to the document that has the information relating to the late nature photographer and rock climber Galen Rowell. In this case, we set a value for the field "`died`".

```
db.people.update ({"name" : "Rowell"}, { "$set": {"died" :
"Bishop"}})
```

`$set` is an example of a **modifier**. It allows us to specify how we want to change the document. In the previous example, the value of the field "`died`" would have been updated or created if it did not yet exist.

Some of the other modifiers are `$unset`, to remove a field, `$inc` and `$dec` to increment and decrement a field, and `$push` and `$pull` to add an element to an array or remove it:

```
mongoDB db.people.findOne({"name" : "Rowell"})
{
  "_id" : ObjectId("54ad46f6812ce43efb530a0a"),
  "name" : "Rowell",
  "first" : "Galen",
  "profession" : "photographer",
  "born" : "Oakland CA",
  "died" : "Bishop"
}
```

MongoDB data types

In MongoDB, we do not have to specify data types ahead of time. You just use them, and by now, you should have recognized, from our examples, the same data types that make up a JSON object. However, in MongoDB we have a few extras.

Basic data types

We can use the same basic data types as in JSON: `null`, `true`, `false`, `string`, `number`, and `array`.

Dates

Dates are always hard to deal with, not only in life but also in databases. Fortunately, MongoDB supports the JavaScript `Date()` class, giving us a data type when using dates. Dates are stored as the number of milliseconds that have elapsed since the epoch and do not contain any information on the time zone. Of course, if you like, you could store the time zone as a separate key:value pair:

```
{ "today" : new Date() }
```

In MySQL, the equivalent of the previous code would be to use `NOW()`. If you issue a `find()` on the document where you added `"today"`, you will see something like:

```
"today" : ISODate("2015-01-14T08:37:17.086Z")
```

Embedded documents

The value of a field in a document can also be an entire document. We called these **embedded documents**.

```
{ "key" : { "name":"Schwarzenegger","first":"Arnold",
"profession":"governator" } }
```

One more example

Let's finish this section on the MongoDB shell with one more example. Let's take our `practical.json` file from *Chapter 10, XML and JSON*, and the JSON object it contains. By simply surrounding it with `db.junelake.insert()`, we can turn it into a MongoDB command:

```
db.junelake.insert ({
  "photocollection": {
    "title": "June Lake",
    "overview": "The June Lake Loop begins  ...",
    "photo": [
      {
        "scaption": "June Lake in the Fall",
        "caption": "June Lake and Carson Peak in the fall",
        "story": "Each time that unfortunate day  ...",
        "smallimg": "imagessmall/junelakefall.jpg",
        "largeimg": "imagespng/junelakeinthefall.png"
      },
      {
        "scaption": "Aspen by Silver Lake",
        "caption": "Aspen trees by Silver Lake",
        "story": "In 1998, I hit the right week of the  ...",
```

```
          "smallimg": "imagessmall/silverlakeaspenfall98.jpg",
          "largeimg": "imagespng/silverlakeaspenfall98.png"
       },
       {
          "scaption": "Gull Lake in the Fall",
          "caption": "Gull Lake in the Fall - Happy fishermen !",
          "story": "If you take the north shore road around ...",
          "smallimg": "imagessmall/gulllake648.jpg",
          "largeimg": "imageslarge/gulllake648.jpg"
       },
       {
          "scaption": "Silver Lake",
          "caption": "Silver Lake - June Lake Loop",
          "story": "Any time of the year, there ...",
          "smallimg": "imagessmall/silver2.jpg",
          "largeimg": "imagespng/silver2.png"
       }
     ]
   }
});
```

Once executed, either by typing it in or storing it in a file first, and then using the `load()` function, we have now inserted a document into the `junelake` collection of our gallery database. We can even access it as a JSON object and walk through it:

```
var json = db.junelake.findOne()

print (json.photocollection.title)
June Lake
```

We can use the `print()` function to display those values. We can even go through a loop, as we did in *Chapter 10, XML and JSON*. That is why I picked the name `json` as my variable name, where we had `json` as the variable that contained what our Ajax call returned:

```
for (var i in json.photocollection.photo) {
print(json.photocollection.photo[i].scaption) }
This will produce the following output:
June Lake in the Fall
Aspen by Silver Lake
Gull Lake in the Fall
Silver Lake
```

So, we might as well, now that we can get JSON straight out of our MongoDB database, use the exact same JavaScript code to generate an HTML page of our photo gallery, right? Wrong! Our database resides on a server and is also the server where we execute the MongoDB shell (even if it is on our developer machine, it still has the role of a server).

In order for that JavaScript code generating our HTML to be useful, it has to be executed on the client and interpreted by a different JavaScript interpreter than the MonoDB shell - the one that we have been using since the beginning of this book: *the browser.*

To paraphrase a famous line out of a James Bond movie: *JSON, how the hell are we going to get this data over here?* Well, this will have to happen the same way like before. We will use an Ajax call to execute code on the server to extract data from our database, this time a MongoDB database, and then process that data on the client side to generate our HTML.

Up to this point, the only programming language we know we can use on the server side is PHP, so we need a way to access our MongoDB database using PHP.

MongoDB and PHP

We will dive right into it. We finished the previous section by inserting documents into the database containing the data we need for our photo gallery page. Then we discovered that we could not use it right away. However, we can, if we have the PHP driver installed and the mongo extension specified in our `php.ini` file, we can access our MongoDB database from a PHP program on the server. It can be extremely short.

Getting our gallery data

This is all it takes:

```php
<?php
$connection = new Mongo();
$db = $connection->gallery;
$junelake = $db->junelake;
$gallery = $junelake->findone();
$jsongallery = json_encode($gallery);
echo $jsongallery;
?>
```

Thanks to the driver, we have access to a `Mongo()` class. On the first line, we make a connection to MongoDB, on the second, we select the database we want to use, and on the third, we specify the collection we are dealing with.

Next, we use the `findone()` method, which we recognize from the previous section. As PHP does not know about JSON objects, this is going to return something else: an array. Now, remember that there is a PHP function that converts an array to JSON: `json_encode()`. There it is. Just `echo` it for the Ajax call to catch it and do the rest of the job on the client side. Here are the other pieces. I have not repeated the CSS file here.

This is the HTML file:

```html
<!doctype html>
<html lang="en">
<head>
<meta charset="utf-8" />
<title>June Lake Gallery</title>
<link href="styles/practical.css" rel="stylesheet" type="text/css"
media="screen"/>
</head>
<script src="./js/jquery-1.10.1.js"></script>
<body>
<div id="mysite">
</div>
</body>
</html>
<script src="./js/practicalmongo.js"></script>
```

This is the JavaScript file:

```javascript
$(document).ready (function () {
$.post( "mongogallery.php", function( json ) {

var html = '<div id="overview"><h1>' + json.photocollection.title
+ '</h1>';
html += '<p>' + json.photocollection.overview + '</p></div>';
html += '<div id="gallery">';

for (var i in json.photocollection.photo)
{
html += '<div class="storybook"><div class="smallmat"><div
class="simage"><a href="';
var scaption = json.photocollection.photo[i].scaption;
var caption = json.photocollection.photo[i].caption;
var largeimg = json.photocollection.photo[i].largeimg;
var smallimg = json.photocollection.photo[i].smallimg;
var story = json.photocollection.photo[i].story;
html += largeimg;
```

```
html += '"><img class="sphoto" src="';
html += smallimg;
html += '" title="';
html += caption;
html += '"></img></a></div><div class="scaption">';
html += scaption;
html += '</div></div><div class="story">';
html += story;
html += '</div></div>';
}
html += '</div>';
$('#mysite').html(html);
}, "json");
});
```

We used the `.post()` jQuery method to execute our PHP script on the server and collect the JSON data. Notice the extra `"json"` argument in the `.post()` statement. It is very important as it tells the Ajax call to expect the data to be in the JSON format, and to not attempt to process it as HTML. If you forget this part, strange things will happen, or worse, nothing at all.

CRUD operations with MongoDB and PHP

We conclude this chapter with an overview on how to perform some of the basic CRUD operations using PHP and MongoDB.

As we have mentioned, PHP does not support JSON objects, so we have to use arrays. In the previous example, we fetched data from the database, so we did not even have to look at the array, we just converted it to JSON. The only disappointing part may be that as we are dealing with a document database that contains JSON objects, we grab data, it shows up as arrays, and we have to convert it back to JSON. That does not appear to be very efficient, but if you already know PHP, it is easy to write.

We will discuss a JSON all the way (JavaScript all the way too) alternative in the final chapter of this book.

Insert documents

Let's add another famous California person to our `people` collection in the `california` database. Those of you familiar with Venice Beach know who I am talking about. He is the guy with a turban on rollerblades, skating up and down the boardwalk. He has not changed in 30 years, except that he is now selling T-shirts instead of cassette tapes.

It is very much the same as the insert() in the MongoDB shell, except our *key:value* pairs are now *key=>value* pairs as part of an associative array:

```php
<?php
$connection = new Mongo();
$db = $connection->california;
$people = $db->people;
$californiadude = array(
'first' => 'Harry', 'name' => 'Perry', 'address' => 'Boardwalk',
'city' => 'Venice', 'state' => 'CA','zip' => '90291', 'song' =>
'Invaders from another Planet'
);
$people->insert($californiadude);
?>
```

Update documents

Let's update our document by adding one more key:value pair:

```php
$people->update(array('name' => 'Perry'),
array('$set' => array('vehicle' => 'rollerblades')));
```

So far, we could have used double quotes instead of single quotes in our examples, but for the $set modifier we can only use single quotes, because, as you know, $ has a special meaning in PHP—without the single quotes, $set would have been interpreted as a PHP variable.

Queries with conditions

Just as we did with the shell, we can use the findone() function to query a document:

```php
$result = $people->findone(array('name' => 'Perry'));
print_r($result);  // in case we want to check our insert was
succesful.
```

Once again, an array is used instead of a key:value pair. But we can make these queries more complex. Several keywords exist that can be use to refine our query. Here is one more example:

```php
$result = $people->findone(array('first' => 'John' , 'age'
=> array ( '$gt' => 50)));
// look for all people named John that are over 50. This is just
an example. Nothing will
// be returned.
```

findone() only gives us one document back and does so as an associative array, like in our very first example. If we use find(), the data of several documents is returned. In the shell we had a nice little output, defaulting to the first 20 documents, but, here, using PHP, we will be given what is called a MongoDB **cursor**.

MongoDB cursor object

The MongoDB db.collection.find() returns all documents as an iterable object, or cursor. In PHP, find() returns all documents with all their data, which is probably not what you want. But, as we do not have too much data at this point, here is one way to get it all and walk or iterate through it in PHP:

```php
<?php
 $connection = new Mongo();
 $db = $connection->california;
 $people = $db->people;
$cursor = $people->find();
foreach ($cursor as $document)
{
    echo $document['name'];  // we could do more of course
}
?>
```

In the example, $cursor is an object of the MongoDB cursor class. Several methods are available for this class, giving you alternate ways to iterate through your cursor. If you want to turn the cursor into an array, you can use the iterator_to_array() function.

In the example, we iterate through $cursor using a foreach() loop, giving us access to each document as an array to do with it whatever we want. What we did was echo the name.

To conclude, we'll show you how to refine our query. Imagine you want to perform the same query, which in SQL would look like:

```sql
SELECT first, last FROM people WHERE age > 50 LIMIT 10;
```

In MongoDB PHP lingo, this would be:

```php
$cursor =              // the variable that will contain the cursor we can
iterate through
$people->find(  // our collection, equivalent to a table
array('age' => array ('$gt '=> 50 ),  // criteria for our query
array ('name' => 1, 'first' => 1, '_id' => 0 ))
 // MongoDB calls this a projection:  which fields we want
)->limit(10);                          // cursor modifier
```

This should, by now, look pretty straightforward to you. The cursor modifier part allows you to limit or influence the data that is returned, for example, there is a **sort** modifier.

The projection array allows you to specify which fields you are interested in. By default, the value of id is always returned, so if you do not need it, add _id => 0 to your projection array.

Summary

In this chapter, you learned about MongoDB, a document database that is very popular amongst NoSQL databases. Documents stored in the database are basically nothing more than JSON objects. They can be grouped in collections, the equivalent of tables in RDBMS.

Using the MongoDB shell, we can populate databases and collections from the command line. From within web applications, we can access a MongoDB database on the server using PHP. This is really easy because JSON objects can be written as associative arrays.

In the last few chapters, there was a lot of sample code and I promised you a textbook so you can learn away from the computer. In the next chapter, there will be a lot more reading to do.

The newest trends in web development are being discussed, triggered by the totally different way people are using the Web compared to just a couple of years ago. We are going to focus a little more on how your website looks and a little less on how it works.

12
Mobile First, Responsive Design with Progressive Enhancement

This is most definitely the chapter with the longest title. There is also a lot of text inside the first part of this chapter, as you will find little or no code examples there. Here, we discuss the newest trends in web development, what is causing it, and what it replaces.

Responsive design

A viewport, or the section of the screen where your browser is, comes in all kinds of sizes. Some are very small, such as the screen of your smartphone, and some can be very large. When I looked at my old website on a screen a lot larger than the one I was used to work on, it was so ugly that I decided to completely redo it using a **responsive design**.

Designing a web page with a fixed width specified in pixels today really is out of the question, as is making several versions of your website to accommodate all these sizes.

In responsive design — I am always tempted to call it responsible design — one does not start off with a canvas of, let us say, 960 px wide and build a site that way, chopping it into fixed size `<div>` blocks. As soon as the view port is smaller than 960px, a part of the site would not be visible and, maybe worse, when the screen is really big, everything around your 960x wide rectangle will look boring and empty. This is simply not done today.

A good design should adjust, respond, to the screen size and always look good. To have a good responsive design, you need to:

- Use a flexible grid: have your building blocks sit side by side when there is room, stack them on top of each other when there is none, and proportionally adjust sizes to do so

- Use percentages, not pixels, in your CSS when you define those sizes

- Use media queries to specify different properties for different screen sizes, resolutions, orientations, and so on

- Use flexible images and fonts

This seems like a lot of work. The good news is that others have already done that hard work for you. There are several CSS/JavaScript frameworks available that feature all the things we just listed. You will simply have to add media queries, customized to your site. The hardest part is probably which framework to choose, as there are several really good ones, in particular **Bootstrap** and **Foundation**.

We have chosen for Foundation and that will be the topic of the next chapter. That choice was a matter of taste or preference. *De gustibus non disputandum!*

Déjà vu

As I am writing this, I am having a flashback-like experience. In my first job in the software industry, I was responsible for porting a software package, TEN/PLUS, to several different flavors of UNIX. Its main component was a full-screen editor.

A full screen in those days was that of a so called **dumb terminal** with 24 lines holding 80 characters each. Then came the **X Window System** and monitors in graphics mode, with icons and many utilities, support for a mouse, and so on. One of those utilities is **xterm**, an X client emulating a dumb terminal. That of course meant you could run full screen editors inside it. But you could resize the xterm window, to be one with more lines or longer lines.

So I had to modify our software to adjust to that size and still be a full-screen editor inside xterm, even if it was 64 lines by 120 characters. This was responsive design 25 years ago! And in 2015 people are still using editors such as vi, emacs, nano, and so on inside terminal windows.

Media queries

The keyword **media** has been in use from the very beginning in HTML and CSS, but it was basically limited to specifying media="print" or media="screen" inside the <link> tag where you specified your CSS file, or by using @media screen inside the CSS file itself.

As of CSS3 and HTML5, we can use media queries in more sophisticated ways, to have specific styling that is applied only when certain conditions are met. Although the media attribute can still be used inside the <link> tag, we recommend you use them inside your CSS files. Media queries are essential to responsive design and, even though we promised you little or no work thanks to available frameworks, it is essential to know how to write or read them.

Here is a typical media query:

```
@media only screen and (orientation: portrait) and (min-width:
480px) and (max-width: 690px) {  /* your rules here */  }
```

In between the curly braces, you would write the styling that is applicable to viewports that are between 480 and 690 pixels wide and your device is in portrait mode. Everything that came before will apply. Everything that is between those curly braces will override what came before.

Here are some of the most common keywords that can be used in media queries:

- **width**: Width of display area
- **height**: Height of display area
- **device-width**: Width of device
- **device-height**: Height of device
- **orientation**: Orientation of device (portrait or landscape)
- **resolution**: Density of pixels, expressed as dpi or dpcm

All, except for orientation of course, can be preceded by minimum or maximum.

Starting the media query with the word only is a handy way to deal with browsers that do not support these newer media queries. It will be silently ignored.

The difference between width and height and the equivalent values prefixed by device should be easy to understand: width and height refer to the size of the browser viewport, whereas device-width and device-height refer to the dimensions of the monitor. Not everybody runs his or her browser full-screen, so width and height are the measurements that you need to use. There is one big caveat though.

Mobile browsers fill the available screen, so you might expect width and device-width to be the same. Unfortunately, that's not always the case. Most smart-phones set the width to a nominal value approximately 1,000 pixels wide (for an iPhone, it's 980 pixels). You have seen several adds of mobile phones showing a full page of the New York Times on the tiny phone. That's why!

With the fine retina displays of today, you would even be able to read the paper that way. But if you worked hard in getting your media queries right for various devices and have one for, let's say `max-width:480px`, your beautiful responsive design will not show up on that mobile phone. Fortunately, there is a remedy for this. Simply put the following line in the `<head>` section of your page:

```
<meta name="viewport" content="width=device-width,
initial-scale=1.0">
```

Now we are truly on our way to a responsive design. By using media queries, we can create a page with a single design that will show elements on the page (think `<div>`) next to each other on a large screen, show them stacked on top of each other on a tablet in portrait mode, and show fewer of them on a mobile phone.

Using the media attribute

You have probably seen sites containing a line like this in the `<head>` section:

```
<link rel="stylesheet" type="text/css" href="print.css"
media="print">
```

It uses the `media` attribute to indicate if this stylesheet needs to be used. In HTML4 this was basically `screen` or `print`. In HTML5 the media attribute can have a lot more values. Those can be the same as what we put after `@media` only on our examples. So if we wanted, we could organize our CSS code in separate stylesheets, one for each media type and use them as appropriate, as is shown in the following example:

```
<link rel="stylesheet" type="text/css" href="small.css"
media="screen and (max-width:480px)">
```

Do more with less

This term probably brings back bad memories to people who lived through the period before and during the financial crisis, but that is not what we are going to talk about.

Now that we have introduced media queries, we are at risk of having to write a lot more CSS, one set of rules for each media query we decide to use. Assume we divide it like three T-shirt sizes: small, medium, large. Add to that portrait and landscape flavors of each: you now have six.

Imagine that someone in the marketing department decides to change the corporate color: you now have to make six changes to your stylesheet.

This is where extensions to CSS, such as **less** (**SASS** is another one) prove to be very handy. One of its features is the use of **variables**. Create a .less file to hold your stylesheet information. Use a variable to hold the color information:

```
@mycolor: #FFDEAD;
```

Inside your media queries, wherever you need to specify this color, use:

```
color: @mycolor;
```

Imagine you want to change it to teal. Just replace that single line by:

```
@mycolor: teal;
```

Bingo! You have changed your color in all six places. Isn't that nice?

Less has more features such as mixins, nested rules, media queries, and more, resulting in better structured and easier to maintain stylesheets. It is all described very clearly at lesscss.org. The name of the site immediately explains why they call it less: You will end up writing less CSS. Just look at these two examples. The following is the less code:

```
@mycolor: #FFDEAD;
@mygreen: teal;
#content {
  background-color: @mycolor;
  .greenp {
  color: @mygreen;
  font-size:12px;
  font-family:Avenir, sans-serif;
  }
  .thumb {
  border: 2px solid @mygreen;
  width:150px;
  }
}
```

This will be translated into the following CSS. And if you really start nesting, this can become a lot more:

```css
#content {
  background-color: #FFDEAD;
  }
#content  .greenp {
  color: teal;
  font-size:12px;
  font-family:Avenir, sans-serif;
  }
#content  .thumb {
  border: 2px solid teal;
  width:150px;
}
```

Let's have one more example with media queries. We could write:

```css
@medium: 16px;
@portraitfont: "Avenir, sans-serif";
.container {
@media screen {
  background-color:@mycolor;
  @media (min-width:786px) {
    font-size:@medium;
    @media (orientation:landscape) {
      margin:auto;
          }
    @media (orientation:portratit) {
      font-family:@portraitfont;
          }
        }
      }
    }
```

This will be translated into the following CSS. Don't you think the less version is less verbose?

```css
@media screen {
    .container {
    background-color:#FFDEAD;
    }
}
@media screen and (min-width:786px) {
    .container {
```

```
        font-size:16px;
      }
  }
@media screen and (min-width:786px) and (orientation:landscape) {
    .container {
      margin:auto;
      }
  }
@media screen and (min-width:786px) and (orientation:portrait) {
    .container {
      font-family:Avenir, Verdana, sans-serif;
      }
  }
```

Now how do we convert the less file to CSS content? There are two ways to do this. When we reach the production stage, we want to use a compiler to generate the CSS file from our less file. In *Chapter 14, Node.js,* you will learn about Node.js and node modules. There is a `node` module for less.

For now, while we are still developing and experimenting more with less, download `less.js` from the `lesscss.org` site.

Inside the `<head>` section of your page, list your less file in a `link` tag:

```
<link rel="stylesheet/less" type="text/css"
href="less/mystyles.less"></link>
```

I like to keep my `less` files in a `less` folder. In the right spot on your page, for example, right before the closing `</body>` tag, add:

```
<script src="js/less.js"></script>
```

Now your `less` file will be converted to CSS on-the-fly, each time the page is loaded. Note that, when editing your `less` files, not all editors will give you the nice color coding and formatting they feature when you edit CSS files. I use Textastic to edit my `less` files. To paraphrase the governator: *You have to watch this editor: it is fantastic!*

Mobile first

Now that we covered how to make our design responsive and make our page look good on screens of all sizes, you might think we have covered mobile devices as well. Nope.

Supporting mobiles is not just about screen sizes. You may have seen the add we talked about where a guy is reading the *New York Times* on his iPhone, a full page spread. This is how mobile devices will render websites on high- resolution displays, unless you tell them not to. Before we continue this thread, I would like to stress that this discussion is about how to design **web applications** that are interpreted by mobile browsers, not native iOS or Android apps.

Why mobile first?

Let's reply with a question: why not? Or let's answer it: because mobile *is* first. Mobile devices (smart-phones and tablets) have been shipping 4-5x more units than PCs or TVs for several years now. More users are visiting the Web using a mobile connection than with fixed Internet access. That is why it is important to think first what experience these mobile users will have when they visit our site and not create a fixed canvas version of a site first and then make changes to deal with mobile users. That would be another case of (not so) *graceful degradation*.

You may not always have the choice if your marketing person shows up with yet another static design from the design firm. But marketing people like numbers, so tell them to check the numbers and you may have a soul mate soon.

We have come a long way

In 2007, not all that long ago, I was developing a modest website with my photographs. A friend of mine was checking it out on his smartphone. After seeing this, I had to buy one myself, not because it was so great but because I needed one to test my website; at least, that was my justification. Even though I could not really afford it, I got the latest greatest Nokia, a brick compared to today's iPhone, that you could flip open to give you a bigger screen and a real keyboard. But the web access on it was terrible. It took what seemed like forever to get a browser started. The little keyboard was OK but the experience is quite different today when I use my iPhone or iPad with a sturdy Bluetooth keyboard. As a matter of fact, a lot of this book was written on an iPad while sitting on the train.

The year before I made several trips back to Belgium and, because my parents had no Internet at home, I went to a so-called Internet hotspot to check my e-mails. For 10 Euros an hour, you could buy a scratchcard that revealed an access code that you needed to use on the local carrier's website together with your cell phone number; then they sent you a password by SMS. This whole procedure would sometimes take 20 minutes and cost me international roaming charges because I had a U.S. phone number. Now I had 40 minutes worth of Wi-Fi left to myself. Mobile Internet was slow and expensive.

Now most of these barriers are gone, bandwidth is up, Wi-Fi is free in most places, or you can install a SIM card.

To take the term *We have come a long way* one step further, allow me to share one little anecdote. I am a big fan of the Eastern Sierra and have taken many trips there, most of the time going through Yosemite National Park. I know a nice alternate road to take you to the West entrance of the Park that goes through the Gold Country town of Coulterville.

The local Jeffery Hotel has a saloon with two signs above the entrance door. One says: *"Magnolia Saloon - est. 1851 - California's Oldest Operating Saloon"*. The one right above it says: *Free WiFi*.

Mobile devices have newer capabilities

The situation described in the last few paragraphs — except for the saloon — has definitely turned around. Mobile devices perform well, Internet access is affordable, and the majority of the devices used can access the World Wide Web, so we better make sure people can access our site or applications with them.

I am not in the habit of using a lot of numbers, I have only used a few so far, but in a recent survey I learned that, of mobile phone users, 84% use them while at home, 63% while in the office, and 42% while on the move.

On mobile devices, there is no clicking with the mouse and no hovering on a phone or tablet, but there is **swiping**. There are many new interfaces, often tied to hardware and iOS that you will not find on desktops. The interface to select a date on a phone is different than, for example, using the jQuery UI date picker.

If you read the specs of the latest greatest iPhone on the Apple website, I bet you they forgot to mention one important feature of the product, at least not in a very visible and obvious way: you can make phone calls with it. So if the contact information of your site contains phone numbers, let the user make a phone call by just clicking that number. It is as easy as putting an <a> tag around it:

```
<a href="tel:6505555555">6505555555</a>
```

This may be a trivial example, but it illustrates mobile first thinking. And the phone will do the rest. So make sure that, when an application is used on a mobile with one of these new capabilities, it can be used.

Mobile devices are not only used while on the road

Forget screen sizes, think content. It is not about small versus large, but about mobile versus local, about on-the-road versus at home. When someone is traveling and is looking for his hotel, he expects to quickly find contact info when he checks the hotel's website on his mobile, not photographs of the rooms and the indoor and outdoor pool. But he may have used that same mobile, while sitting in his couch at home to make the reservation, because the kids were using the computer or iPad. So on that day he was interested in those pictures.

So if he is looking for the hotel we could, if the phone supports it, show him a map on his smart phone, in a GPS-like fashion, showing his location as well as that of his hotel.

What we do not want to do is to make his cellular phone carrier wealthy by forcing a download of 900x600 JPG files in areas where bandwidth is poor yet expensive, because someone decided to have a photo banner on the home page at any given time.

Content first, navigation next

The previous comments boil down to this. In our thinking, we should put the most important content within immediate reach. Having a horizontal menu with *contact* all the way to the right or, worse, somewhere at the bottom of the page is not going to help our traveler.

In a recent project where I had to deal with a design firm's wireframe made for a desktop screen, containing a horizontal navigation, I looked at all the navigation items and rearranged them, contact first, replaced the photo banner with responsive images and replaced that menu with the word `menu` with three stripes underneath.

I placed most of my code inside my `max-width:480px` media query. A simple tab on `menu` would present the visitor with a menu on the small screen with all the relevant topics.

The way I did this, the menu will appear to be coming from the left of your phone somewhere, similar to what the Facebook app does. I used **Foundation** to achieve that. You will learn about Foundation in the next chapter.

Small means big

You may have noticed on many sites, even really good ones, that you are being switched to a mobile version of the site, a different URL like `m.site.com`, while visiting them on your smart-phone. This is not what we recommend. Once you decide to go with two, what is to stop you from creating a third, and so on? Many web designers who stay with a single site react to smaller by shrinking everything down so things still fit on the screen.

In many cases, you may want to do the opposite because it is going to become hard to read. Retina screens and the like are so crisp these days that smaller typefaces on these screens are actually easy to read. You could do both by handling the Retina or not question in a media query.

On the other hand, this is an as-good-as-ever moment to point out that, of these millions of new people accessing the Web on mobiles, many are of an older generation who would appreciate a bigger font size because their eyes are not what they used to be.

The real issue is not the text but that you do not have the pixel-level accuracy of a mouse. When you want to click on something you will have to use your finger. If these areas are shrunk down as well, the risk of clicking on the wrong thing goes up dramatically.

Mobile input

We mentioned reading, we mentioned clicking, how about filling out a web form? A lot of old-school websites — for example, web shops containing registration forms — have many `<input>` fields and are designed to fit on a full screen with a single *submit* button at the end. So, on a phone this is going to be hard; therefore you may want to consider splitting up these forms. If the input field is not big enough, tapping with a finger may take the user to the wrong spot. So you want to make these bigger than on a desktop. But there is one other thing about input that is often forgotten: the keyboard.

On a smart phone or tablet, there is no keyboard. When the web application/browser detects that input is needed, a soft keyboard shows up as part of your screen. On a smart phone in portrait mode, that makes it hard to type.

When there is a need to type in a number, you need to first switch that keyboard to a different mode, and yet another mode for some symbols. Not everybody is schlepping a Bluetooth keyboard with him everywhere he goes, like I do. For this part, you can use the new `<input>` types in HTML5. Most mobile browsers are HTML5-capable so when you use the following:

```
<input type="email" name="email"></input>
```

Those browsers will present you with a keyboard layout that has at least the @ sign in it, which on some keyboards is hard to find. I live in *azerty* country again. I know.

Mobile first recap

You probably get the picture. In this new world with millions of mobile devices, we need a new way of thinking about what information we provide on our site and how we do that. Use features of the phone, when you can; put content before navigation. Design your site as *one site fits all*, not *one size fits all*. This is not a technology, but a philosophy.

But we will need a technology to determine whether the browser/device combination supports certain features, such as **geolocation**, or even interprets JavaScript, and use it only when present. When we do that, we are practicing **progressive enhancement**.

Progressive enhancement

A few years ago, a colleague once told our project manager that 80% of the time he spent changing already finished code to make it work in old browsers. In those days, a lot of people spent a lot of time making *round corners* work on Internet Explorer in a costly (in terms of development time and performance) attempt to make everything look exactly the same everywhere. A lot of folks decided to postpone adapting the new features in CSS3 and HTML5 because some browsers did not support them. This was just to support a single digit number of browsers and make sure the website was still functional when you switched off JavaScript (graceful degradation).

Today, there is bad news and there is good news. The bad news is that there are more browsers than you can imagine and a lot of browser/device pairs support APIs that others don't. The good news is that several technologies have emerged to tackle this problem in a more proactive or, shall I say, progressive way.

So how do we handle this and still come up with a single version of our site? First, we need another philosophical change: do not be afraid to use the features that are available, make your sites and applications more cool and exciting, and enhance them with those features. How will we handle browsers or devices that do not support those features?

We propose a two-stage process. First, we will determine what the minimal content of our site has to be if virtually no modern features (for example JavaScript, fancy CSS features, and media queries) are available and start by writing our page accordingly. This is our basic site. Next we will add things such as jQuery and JavaScript code, media queries, and newer CSS and HTML features, animation, and so on to make our site nicer, to enhance it. This is called progressive enhancement.

Once again, there is jQuery and another library, called **EnhanceJS**, to help us do that. We will illustrate how. After that we show how to refine this technique: test for a particular feature, use it if available, and possibly use a replacement library or polyfill that adds the feature to non-capable browsers. We already used such a polyfill in a previous chapter — the history plugin for jQuery.

EnhanceJS

EnhanceJS will test the browser for a comprehensive set of features. If they all pass, we load the files that make up the enhanced version of our site, such as jQuery, a CSS file with media queries, and so on. If not, the site that we look at is our basic site.

Please note, if we want to use Ajax to dynamically inject HTML into parts of our page, we will not be able to do this in the basic version. Depending on how much content we decide we want on there, it may be "Back to the future" all over again, as we will have to provide links to static pages. That way, all our visitors using old equipment will see at least a functional site with reasonable content.

Look at this example:

```
<!DOCTYPE html>
<html>
<head>
<meta charset=utf-8" />
<title>Progressive Hello World</title>
<link href="css/basic.css" type="text/css" rel="stylesheet" />
<script type="text/javascript" src="js/enhance.js"></script>
<script type="text/javascript">
  // Run capabilities test
  enhance({
  loadScripts: [
    'js/jquery.min.js',
    'js/enhanced.js'
    ],
  loadStyles: ['css/enhanced.css']
    });
</script>
</head>
<body>
<div id="content"><h1>Hello, world</h1></div>
</body>
</html>
```

enhance.js

enhance.js is a JavaScript library that performs a comprehensive suite of tests to see whether the browser supports enough features to handle what you had in mind for your enhanced site. At the time of writing, one could find it at `https://code.google.com/p/enhancejs`. You can also find documentation there and useful links.

If the test fails, nothing inside `enhance()` will happen and your basic site, in our example good ol' *Hello World*, will be what the visitor sees. If the test succeeds, enhance.js will add the class `enhanced` to the `<html>` tag and attempt to perform the tasks you put inside it.

loadStyles and loadScripts

loadStyles and **loadScripts** are two arrays where you can specify which stylesheets and JavaScript files you want to load. You can also specify conditions such as media queries to conditionally load one file or another. Instead of placing simply the pathname of the files in your array, you could use a JavaScript object using attribute names as the keys. So in our first example, we could have written:

```
enhance({
  loadScripts: [
    { src: 'js/jquery.min.js'},
    { src: 'js/enhanced.js'  }
    ],
  loadStyles: [
    { href: 'css/enhanced.css' }
    ]
});
```

Here is a more elaborate example:

```
enhance({
  loadStyles: [
    {media: 'screen', href: 'js/mediumlarge.css',
    excludemedia: 'screen and (max-device-width: 480px)',},
    {media: 'screen and (max-device-width: 480px)', href: 'js/small.
css'}
    ],
  loadScripts: [
    {media: 'screen', src: 'js/mediumlarge.js',
    excludemedia: 'screen and (max-device-width: 480px)'},
    {media: 'screen and (max-device-width: 480px)', src: 'js/small.
js'}
    ]
});
```

enhanced and FOUC

There is a common problem known as **Flash of unstyled content (FOUC)** — be careful how you spell the acronym. This is the phenomenon where your see some flickering on your screen caused by temporarily displaying your HTML that is not yet processed by your JavaScript code during page load. There is an opportunity here to tackle this problem based on the knowledge that, if the enhance.js test is successful, it will add the class enhanced to the <html> tag.

In our example, you could add the following to your **enhanced.css** and **enhanced.js** respectively:

```
#content {
html.enhanced display:none;
}

$('#content').show(); // this of course at the end of the
processing
```

The above statement almost implies that, in the enhanced version of the site, we have code in our enhanced.js that will result in HTML being injected inside the #content div. Another approach would be to have #basiccontent div and #enhancedcontent div and make only the one that is appropriate visible.

Enhance.js, as described here, gives us an all-or-nothing approach. It runs a comprehensive set of tests to determine whether the visitor should see the basic version or the enhanced version. They are described in the documentation and of course in the code of enhance.js itself. At the time of writing, enhance.js had not been updated since 2010. There is nothing wrong with that: it does a job that has not changed and it does it well.

None of these tests check support for some of the newer HTML5 and CSS3 features such as **Canvas**. Enhance.js has more configurable options that allow you to add your own tests and, if you like, run enhance() more than once to test different conditions. So you could do it that way.

 There really is no need to because, as is often the case in the world of web development, an entire team has done this for us already.

Modernizr

Modernizr.js is similar to Enhance.js, it is a JavaScript library that tests browsers for features. But it has a lot more tests, can be customized, and can be used at a more granular level than Enhance.js. Modernizr tests for individual features. Depending on whether the test succeeds (*Yep*) or not (*Nope*), we can load different stylesheets and .js scripts.

You can even use the two together. Start by using enhance.js to determine whether the browser supports JavaScript. If it does, load modernizr.js together with jQuery and refine what you want to do, in your own JavaScript code. Your basic page could look like this:

```
<!DOCTYPE html>
<html class="no-js">
<head>
<meta charset=utf-8" />
<title>My first progressive enhancement site</title>
<link href="css/basic.css" type="text/css" rel="stylesheet" />
<script type="text/javascript" src="js/enhance.js"></script>
<script type="text/javascript">
  enhance({
  loadScripts: [
    'js/jquery.js',
    'js/modernizr.js',
    'js/enhanced.js'
    ],
  loadStyles: ['css/enhanced.css']
    });
</script>
</head>
<body>
<div id="basiccontent"><h1>Welcome to Polbol Productions</h1><p>
Thank you for visiting us. Apparently you cannot use your browser
to access all the
cool goodies on our site. Click <a href="basic.html">here</a> for
more information on our
company.<br/> The Polbol Productions Team</p></div>
<div id="enhancedcontent"> <!-- Your real home page here --> </div>
</body>
</html>
```

So, we have changed it a little bit from the previous section. We of course added the `modernizr.js` library to be part of our JavaScript line-up, but one remarkable tiny change is the `class="no-js"` attribute for the `<html>` tag. Whereas enhance.js adds the class `enhanced` to this tag, Modernizr will replace this class with `js` when it runs. So if it does not, because there is no JavaScript, you can account for it in your stylesheets with the `.no-js` class.

Modernizr will add a lot more classes to the `<html>` tag, almost one for every test passed. So once again you could accommodate them in your stylesheet. Using this example on my MacBook Pro with Firefox as the browser, I checked with Firebug and noticed that modernizr.js had replaced `no-js` with `js` and added the following classes to the `<html>` tag:

```
js flexbox flexboxlegacy canvas canvastext webgl no-touch geolocation
postmessage no-websqldatabase indexeddb hashchange history draganddrop
websockets rgba hsla multiplebgs backgroundsize borderimage
borderradius boxshadow textshadow opacity cssanimations csscolumns
cssgradients no-cssreflections csstransforms csstransforms3d
csstransitions fontface generatedcontent video audio localstorage
sessionstorage webworkers applicationcache svg inlinesvg smil
svgclippaths
```

The Modernizr object

Once you have loaded modernizr.js and all the tests have been performed, you have access to the `Modernizr` object and can check in your JavaScript code whether or not a test has passed:

```
if (Modernizr.history) {
// code to use the HTML5 history API
}
else {
// code to use the API of your history plugin  or polyfill
}
```

Polyfills and Modernizr

Polyfills are scripts that take care of functionality a browser lacks when you need it. The `history.js` library that we discussed at length in *Chapter 9, The History API – Not Forgetting Where We Are*, could be a polyfill for the HTML 5 History API. I said, could, because in our example in that chapter we used history.js regardless. True polyfills are used only when the feature is lacking. So the code above could use a different API if HTML5 support is there compared to the API available through the polyfill.

This could explain why the name Modernizr is chosen. Whereas enhance.js allows you to take care of people using the old stuff and give them an interface using the current stuff, Modernizr allows you to write today the code that your visitor will use tomorrow or next week, when they update their computer or buy a new phone or tablet. You are now ahead of the game.

Your site or application already uses all the cool stuff HTML5 and CSS3 offers and has fallback code in case older technology is involved. You can motivate your customer or visitor to update sooner rather than later, but your site or application already supports what to them lies in the future. Is this cool, or what?

yepnope.js or Modernizr.load

Just like you saw in the *Enhance.js* section, you conditionally load files based on passing or failing a test. The coolest conditional loader is **yepnope.js**. At the time of writing, it was going to be deprecated, so its inclusion inside Modernizr might disappear. For sure, something newer will show up. So, for now, we include a short example of how you can do conditional loading of static assets with Modernizr:

```
Modernizr.load({
  test: Modernizr.geolocation,
   yep : 'geo.js',
   nope: 'geo-polyfill.js'
});
```

Summary

This chapter has the longest title in the book, fitting for the most important one. In it, we explained the difference between web development yesterday and web development tomorrow. We explained that you need to think mobile first, that your design has to be responsive, and that you should reward customers who have the latest, greatest stuff by using the cool new features through progressive enhancement.

In the next chapters, we will guide you through how to apply all that came before using a cool CSS/JavaScript framework, Foundation, so you can use what someone already did for you. We will also show you a way to take full control of how you want things to be handled on the server side, using node.js.

If you stop right here, you have learned the basics of modern web development and I congratulate you for doing that. If you go on, you will learn to use a framework that will save you a lot of time and work in the long run as well as what looks like a totally different way of doing things. As we go on explaining it, you will realize that it is not all that different in the first place.

13
Foundation – A Responsive CSS/JavaScript Framework

I usually describe **Zurb Foundation** and **Twitter Bootstrap** to people as "the thing I always wanted to write but never found the time to do".

One could call them frameworks or not, but I recommend you check the websites of both to learn what they call themselves. I have used both and compared them and have decided to go with **Foundation**. It is a matter of taste. I always like to go with the bigger challenge. I preferred studying Finnish over learning Swedish. You may find Bootstrap easier to use, as it probably contains more widgets, but when I look at a website, it is, in my opinion, easier to recognize that it was developed with Bootstrap out of the box than with Foundation. I have included an overview of Bootstrap as an appendix.

Our responsive toolkit – Foundation

In the previous chapter, you learned all the pieces of the puzzle we need to develop a *mobile first*, progressive enhancement, responsive design web application. Mobile first is a way of thinking; for the progressive enhancement part, we used enhance.js and modernizr.js. So, we still need to know how to do the responsive part by writing a flexible grid, creating media queries, supporting flexible images, and then some.

This is the part that Foundation has already done for us. In addition, it does have some cool User Interface (UI) components. One of them is *off-canvas*, an awesome feature to be used on mobiles and tablets that, since I have used it, I recognize on every major website or app, Facebook included. Check out the excellent Foundation documentation for the full list of features. In this chapter, we will describe the ones that I found particularly useful.

Foundation components

After you download Foundation from `http://foundation.zurb.com/` (I recommend you go with the complete option), you will see that it contains CSS components and JavaScript components. I placed them all in a folder `foundation5` to make it easier to switch releases, or even to maintain a Bootstrap flavor of the site as well.

Here is what you will get with the download:

- **index.html**: This is a web page that shows you the most common features of Foundation.

- **css**: This is a folder containing `foundation.css` and `foundation.min.css`, the Foundation stylesheet. Include one of these in the `<head>` section of your site. In addition, include your own stylesheet. We recommend that you do not modify `foundation.css`. Otherwise, if a new version comes along, you end up overwriting your code.

- **js/foundation.min.js**: This is all of the Foundation JavaScript. Put this right before the end of your `<body>` tag, after jQuery. Also, do not modify this file.

- **js/foundation**: This is a folder containing separate JavaScript source files for the foundation features in case you want to explore how they work. There is no need to include this in your web page.

- **js/vendor**: This is a folder containing more useful JavaScript libraries such as jQuery and **Modernizr**.

Foundation uses Modernizr, so aren't you glad we already know what this is?

Reference `modernizr.js` in the `<head>` section of your site so that all the tests can be performed before the page is loaded. Place `jQuery.js` right before the end of `<body>`, and before `foundation.min.js`. Then, add the following lines, which will start Foundation:

```
<script>
      $(document).foundation();
</script>
```

The grid system

Foundation comes with a grid system that, by default, divides your working screen real estate into 12 columns. Using classes, you specify for every block on the screen how many columns wide you want it to be. There are different classes for different sizes; this is the Foundation way to make responsive design easy.

Imagine a variety of screens and devices you want your website to look great on. Let's look at the larger ones and call them a canvas for a moment. Picture two vertical lines, about 1024px apart, centered on the canvas. These will be the vertical borders of our working area. Of course, once you reduce the size of your viewport, or if you are using a tablet or mobile, your working area is going to be the full width of your screen.

Now, to build the layout of our web page, we are going to divide it into horizontal rows, inside which, we will place responsive blocks (`<div>`) of content. For those, there are classes we can use, indicating what size screen (think of it as what type of T-shirt) we are dealing with, and how many columns we want to fill. Look at the following example:

```
<div class="row">
<div class="small-12 medium-6 large-4 columns">
<h3>First block title</h3>
<p> First block text</p>
</div>
<div class="small-12 medium-6 large-4 columns">
<h3>Second block title</h3>
<p>Second block text</p>
</div>
<div class="small-12 medium-6 large-4 columns">
<h3>Third block title</h3>
<p>Third block text</p>
</div>
</div>
```

So, this was our first `row` of things, containing three responsive blocks. Now, we build mobile first, so the first class we used indicates how many columns wide we want that block to be on a mobile, our small T-shirt. We go for the max: 12. If you do not specify anything for sizes medium and large, they will implicitly inherit the same values. Always include the `columns` class as well.

You've probably already figured out what will be going on here. When you display this on a small screen, every one of these three blocks will be 12 columns wide, which is as far as we can go, so they will be stacked on top of each other. When we switch to medium, like when turning our tablet from vertical to landscape, we will have a row of two and one below it. On large screens, they will all fit next to each other.

Class end

If you do not have enough items in a row to fill all columns, the last item will be placed on the right edge. If you want to override that, you can add a class called end for this, and it will appear where you expected it.

Visibility classes

There is a whole collection of classes that fit right in here that I always had trouble finding in the documentation because they were described before the *Grid* section: **visibility classes**. Similar to determining how many columns wide you want something to be, you may want to decide whether to show it or not, depending on the device. The most popular example is probably the three bar menu icon you see on small screens replacing the horizontal navigation on "normal" size screens. You can choose between hiding and showing for a T-shirt size, or one size and up. The names should speak for themselves. It also shows that we have more sizes in our T-shirt shop.

Even more useful are the classes you can use to say yes or no to show things depending on the orientation of your screen, and whether or not it is a touch-screen device. This is one reason why you should not forget to include modernizr.js. Here is the list:

show-for-touch	show-for-medium-up	hide-for-small-only
hide-for-touch	show-for-large-only	hide-for-medium-only
show-for-landscape	show-for-large-up	hide-for-medium-up
hide-for-landscape	show-for-xlarge-only	hide-for-large-only
show-for-small-only	show-for-xlarge-up	hide-for-large-up
show-for-medium-only	show-for-xxlarge-up	hide-for-xlarge-only
hide-for-xlarge-up	hide-for-xxlarge-up	

The block grid system

This made me pronounce words of wisdom that confused people and will confuse you until you have seen the example: having things that are the same size is not the same as having things be the same size.

The classes that belong to the block grid system allow you to make sure that your item blocks are evenly spaced no matter what screen size. You can do so by specifying how many items you want in a row, not how many columns wide you want an item to be.

As a consequence, your items will become smaller on smaller screens, so they are no longer the same size, but all items in a row will have an equal size, so they all have the same size. Got it? This is a great feature to use in simple photo galleries or blog posts.

You can use the block grid by assigning the class(es) to a `<ul>` element, and your items are the `<li>` elements. A typical class name would be `size-block-grid-number`. For example:

```
<ul class="small-block-grid-2 medium-block-grid-3 large-block-grid-4">
<li><!-- first item here --></li>
....
</ul>
```

Useful UI elements

As mentioned before, Foundation is well-documented, and there are books available if you want to read and learn even more. In the remainder of this chapter, we will go over a select number of UI features I found to be very useful, with a few examples that combine them.

After that, we will finish the chapter with the Foundation way of doing navigation, **on-canvas** and **off-canvas**.

Thumbnails – for simple galleries

Foundation is changing, so at the time of writing this book, there were several UI features to produce image sliders or other cool things to do with photographs that were going to be majorly modified or replaced.

However, everybody needs to have thumbnails of their pictures to be part of the design. In Foundation, there is a simple class called `th` that you can use that will produce a nicely formatted responsive thumbnail with or without a caption. For example:

```
<a class="th" href="/photo.jpg">
<img src="smallimgs/photo.jpg"></img> <div><h6>Caption</h6></div>
</a>
```

This puts nice styling around your thumbnail image and caption, but once you click on it, the larger image will be shown in a way decided by your browser.

Reveal modals – your better pop-up

It would be a lot nicer if our larger image would show up in a nice pop-up. Pop-ups can be used anywhere on a site. Foundation offers what they call **reveal modals**. They are very simple to use.

There is the area on the site where you place something that gives access to the pop-up. In the example, it is a simple `<div>`, not even an `<a>` tag. You give the element a `data-reveal-id` attribute, with the ID of the element you want to reveal as a value.

Next, there is the element that has that ID and contains what you want shown in the pop-up. Note the `<a>` tag at its end with class `close-reveal-modal`. This will trigger the pop-up to disappear when clicked. If you forget this part, there is no way that the user can make the pop-up go away:

```
<div data-reveal-id="revealid">Click here</div>
<div id="revealid"  class="reveal-modal medium" data-reveal >
<p>Text of popup</p><a class="close-reveal-modal">&#215;</a></div>
```

Dropdowns

Maybe you want a drop down (or drop up or drop left) instead of a pop-up.
In this example, we introduce a `button`, Foundation style. We have also returned to the T-shirt shop: both the button and the actual drop down can be given a size class. When you include the `content` class, the drop down will be given some nice padding. There is also an option that you can use to make the drop down show up on hover:

```
<a   class="button tiny" data-dropdown="calpeople"
data-options="is_hover:true">California people</a>
<ul id="calpeople" class="small f-dropdown content"
data-dropdown-content>
      <li>Ansel Adams</li>
      <li>John Muir</li>
      <li>Arnold Schwarzenegger</li>
</ul>
```

Example – a simple photo gallery

Let's now combine a block grid, thumbnails, reveal modals, and a drop down to produce a nice responsive photo gallery. We will use the modal to display the larger image and the drop down to display technical details of the photograph.

This is the code fragment through the first photograph:

```
<div class="row">
<ul class="small-block-grid-3 medium-block-grid-4
large-blockgrid-5" >
<li>
<div class="th" data-reveal-id="tiogalakepf" data-reveal>
<img src="imagessmall/tiogalakesmall.jpg" alt="Tioga Lake">
<div class="caption"><h6>Tioga Lake</h6></div>
</div>
<div id="tiogalakepf"  class="reveal-modal medium portfolio"
data-reveal >
<img src="imageslarge/tiogalake.jpg"></img>
<p>&copy; 1997-2015 Paul Wellens</p>
<h3>Tioga Lake in april of 1997</h3>
<a class="button small" data-dropdown="tiogadrop"
data-options="align:top">Details</a>
<ul id="tiogadrop" class="f-dropdown content"
data-dropdown-content>
    <li>Hasselblad</li>
    <li> Fuji Velvia</li>
    <li> 40mm CF lens </li>
    <li> f16 </li>
</ul>
<a class="close-reveal-modal">&#215;</a>
</div>
</li>
</ul>
</div>
```

Accordions

Accordions are very useful when you have information that is divided into logical sections and you want to expand, and then collapse back, some of the content. I find it a great tool to be used in an online resume, for instance, for job history sections, or for FAQs. I have used it for years with jQuery UI. Since I discovered Foundation, I am using their accordion.

It is very easy to set up; you can use either a `<ul>` element or a `<dl>` element to create your accordion. We are using `<dl>` in our example.

```
<div class="small-12 columns">
<h3>California People</h3>
<dl class="accordion  data-accordion=">
<dd class="accordion-navigation"><a  href="#ansel">
```

```
<h5><i class="fa fa-caret-right green" ></i>Ansel Adams</h5></a>
<div  class="content"  id="ansel">
<p>I think of Ansel Adams as the best landscape photographer ever.
His black and white photographs of Yosemite National Park and New
Mexico are legendary </p>
</div>
</dd>
...
</dl>
```

Awesome Font awesome

In this example, we introduced not only accordions, but also an exciting feature that comes from outside Foundation: Font awesome (www.fontawesome.io). Long gone are the days where you need to have a .gif, .png, or .jpg file for every image that you need on your screen, and a separate one for every size you need.

You can now use icons in your code as if they were HTML elements with a certain class. Under the hood, they are vector images, so they scale well, and as they are HTML elements with a class, you can style them with CSS. There are over 500 icons to choose from. Font awesome uses the <i> tag, deprecated for its original use. So, by adding two classes, fa and fa-caret-right, your <i> becomes a cool right arrow that helps making the accordion more intuitive.

In the example, we gave it an additional class, green, with the matching color in our CSS file. If we click on an item to expand the accordion, we want it to be a blue down arrow. That we do in JavaScript, as follows:

```
$("dl.accordion").on("click", "a", function(e){
var faicons = $(this).parent().parent().find('i.fa');
faicons.removeClass("blue").addClass("green").removeClass("fa-
caret-down").addClass("fa-caret-right");
if ($(this).parent().hasClass("active")) {
  var faicon = $(this).parent().find('i.fa');
  faicon.removeClass("blue").addClass("green").removeClass("fa-
caret-down").addClass("fa-caret-right");
  }
});
```

Foundation uses a class called active to indicate that a part of the accordion was expanded. So, we check for this class before changing the shape and color of our arrow. Of course, we do not know where we were at beforehand, so we started off by changing all arrows to right and green first.

Equalizer – the hardest thing to do with two <div>s made easy

One of the things I find very hard to do is to make sure that two blocks of content that are sitting next to each other always have an equal height. You can, of course, give them an equal height in pixels, but what if the content in one part grows beyond your specified height, and what if that height is higher than the device itself? It would be better not to specify a fixed height and let your <div>s grow with the content, but then how do you make sure they stay aligned?

Equalizer in Foundation will take care of that for you. It may sound like the title of another Arnold Schwarzenegger movie but it is equally powerful. It uses HTML5 data-attributes to get the job done. Simply add `data-equalizer` to the parent container and `data-equalizer-watch` to all the containers you want to be of equal height.

Navigation

There are many more features with Foundation that you want to look at. My intention was to highlight the ones that attracted me so much that I decided to use the framework. One of them was **orbit**, a great slider for photographs, but that one is now deprecated. The Foundation team has recommended an alternative that is pretty cool, but either way, these things would be hard to explain in a textbook. We will give you the whole enchilada in a bonus chapter, which is available online only.

We conclude this chapter with the two main navigation components Foundation offers: one for an **on-canvas menu bar** and another one for an **off-canvas menu**.

Top bar – not just your regular menu bar

Possibly the top shelf of menu bars, the top-bar of Foundation is a very complex piece that gives you everything you might need to create an easy to navigate horizontal menu bar.

Your top shelf is divided in three compartments: the *title* area end, the *left*, and the *right* list of menu items. Here is an example. For the sake of brevity, we did not include any `href` attributes inside the <a> tags:

```
<div class="row">
  <nav class="top-bar" data-topbar role="navigation">
  <ul class="title-area">
   <li class="name">
   <h1><a href="#">My Site</a></h1>
    </li>
```

```
    <!-- Here is the spot to add magic -->
    </ul>

    <section class="top-bar-section">
      <!-- Right Nav Section -->
      <ul class="right">
        <li><a>Overview</a></li>
        <li class="has-dropdown">
          <a>East California</a>
          <ul class="dropdown">
            <li><a>High Sierra</a></li>
            <li><a>Mono Lake</a></li>
            <li><a>June Lake</a></li>
            <li><a>Death Valley</a></li>
          </ul>
        </li>
        <li class="has-dropdown">
          <a>California Coast</a>
          <ul class="dropdown">
            <li><a>Venice Beach</a></li>
            <li><a>Big Sur</a></li>
            <li><a>San Simeon</a></li>
            <li><a>Point Reyes</a></li>
          </ul>
      </li>
      </ul>
      <!-- Left Nav Section -->
      <ul class="left">
      <li><a>About</a></li>
      </ul>
        </section>
      </nav>
    </div>
```

As you can tell, it is relatively straightforward. As is often the case in classical website development, menus are <ul> elements, and menu items are <li> elements. If you want submenus, a class called dropdown can be used and another <ul> underneath. The order of left and right does not matter. This is very nice because that means you can use the same HTML for your basic version. Just add static HTML files as values of an href attribute and do your modern, responsive version with your own cool JavaScript magic.

Foundation created nice styling around top-bar with several shades of dark grey (not fifty), which, of course, you can change in your own CSS file.

Adding more magic

It is magic. By simply adding one `<li>` element to the title area, you can have Foundation create an entire alternate menu for you for tiny screens. Just check this out. Add this to the example where indicated and see what happens when you make the viewing area very small:

```
<li class="toggle-topbar  menu-icon"><a
href="#"><span>Menu</span></a></li>
```

You can leave out the `<span>` element so that only the menu icon will show up or leave out the `menu-icon` class. Obviously, you should not leave out both, otherwise people will not have access to your magic.

Yet more magic – off-canvas, the coolest thing

Place your main menu to the left of your phone until you need it.

I find this the *piece de resistance*, excuse my French, of Foundation. The first time I used it, I was impressed. The next time I went to Facebook, I thought I recognized it in the Facebook app.

The concept is quite simple. In your code, place the content of a menu that should be off-limits at first, to the left. The important thing to control is the section that it should be to the left side of. When a user clicks on the menu button, typically the menu bar icon, a menu will slide in from the left.

This way, we can expand from the previous example. Rather than have Foundation give us a mobile version of our original menu, we can now specify a mobile first menu content. Here is a small example. There will be a larger one in the bonus chapter which we'll be adding online. We also use the visibility classes to make sure that the full-width menu does not appear and is replaced by the menu with the icon. Once you click on it, the left off-canvas will appear next to your content. The height is determined by where you have placed the closing `<div>` tags for off-canvas-wrap and inner-wrap:

```
<div  class="off-canvas-wrap"  data-offcanvas>
 <div class="inner-wrap">
 <div class="row">
 <nav class="tab-bar show-for-small">
 <a class="left-off-canvas-toggle menu-icon ">
 <span>Menu</span>
 </a>
 </nav>
```

```
<div class="left-off-canvas-menu show-for-small">
<ul class="off-canvas-list exit-off-canvas">

<li><label>Portfolios</label></li>
<li><a>High Sierra</a></li>
<li><a>Eastern Sierra</a></li>
<li><a>June Lake</a></li>
<li><a>California Coast</a></li>
</ul>
</div>
<nav class="top-bar hide-for-small" data-topbar>
<ul class="title-area">
<li class="name">
<h1>
<a>My Site</a>
</h1>
</li>
</ul>
<section class="top-bar-section">
<ul class="right">
...
```

Summary

In this chapter, we described the Foundation CSS/JavaScript framework. It allows us to create a mobile first, responsive design site or application without having to write any code for the responsive part. We only have to customize it to our needs.

This concludes the part of the book that covers what I would like to call modern web development. In the final chapter, we advance to what most of us will seem *avant garde*, although by the time this book is printed, it will be very much *en vogue*. And it is all built around a JavaScript thing that is not written in JavaScript called **node.js**.

14
Node.js

Congratulations! You have now made it to the final chapter of this book. After having gone through most of the technologies used in both classical and modern web development, we are now going to discuss the basics of what I would like to call the *avant-garde*, excuse my French, of web development: node.js and friends.

In everything we discussed so far, we used what is often referred to as the **LAMP** (or **MAMP** or **WAMP**, depending on the OS on your server) stack: **Linux Apache MySQL PHP**. Even when we swap out MySQL for **MongoDB**, the acronym still stands. Or we could call it **LANP** with the N of **NoSQL**.

So we had to learn all these languages: JavaScript on the client side, to be interpreted by the browser; PHP, to be interpreted by the Apache web server; and many more. Just imagine you could swap out everything, even things you would not think of — the web server — in favor of JavaScript? That is what node.js does for you. As I, being of a somewhat older generation, see it, node.js did to web development what Schoenberg and Webern did to classical music, Picasso and Braque to painting, and oh well, why not, Venice Beach rappers to pop music.

There is good news and bad news here. The bad news is that we are at risk of having to start everything over again and have learned a lot of things in vain, but the good news is that node.js based solutions *perform* well, *scale* well, and, for those that come after us, only require the knowledge of a single programming language: JavaScript. Acronyms for this are still up for grabs: **LJMJ** or **LNMJ** (J for **JavaScript** or N for **node.js** respectively) or **MEN** (**MongoDB, Express, node.js**)? One that is already used a lot is **MEAN**. Over time people will agree on one. Who invented the word *cubism*?

In this chapter, we will make an attempt to repeat everything you have learned so far while doing things the node.js way. So we already know in which language our code will be written: JavaScript. What we are going to write may come as a surprise to you.

Node.js

Let's recapitulate a bit; in *Chapter 1, The World Wide Web,* you learned about the World Wide Web and how all these millions of pages are accessed by people using a browser that sends requests to a web server using the HTTP protocol. Well, people will still use browsers that send HTTP requests, but we just tossed the web server, now what do we do? We write one. Scary? No, it will be a lot of fun. Writing low-level code is not your thing? No sweat, somebody already did it for you. There is a whole community writing code for node.js that everybody else can use. That code is made available as what is referred to as **modules**, and of course there is a HTTP module available to us.

Another thing the web server did for us was to actually analyze the URL the user typed and explore the **file system** to see whether there is a physical file, for example, an `hello.html` file, and serve it up back to the client. We will have to write that too. This is cool because it will give us full control over what exactly our web server should be able to handle and what it shouldn't. As expected, there are `url` and `fs` modules for node.js as well.

We will need a database but, we already know one that we like: MongoDB. Can we use it with node.js? Yes we can. There is a module or driver for it to access the existing MongoDB server from node.js. As MongoDB is a document database and documents are really JSON objects, this is a perfect fit in an all-JavaScript ecosystem.

Little by little we are beginning to realize, before even having written one, whether a node application is actually going to be a web server that contains application-specific code or an application that contains a web server; take your pick.

As soon as I walk you through our first examples, you will realize that we never before had a need to write so much code for a simple `Hello,  World` program. Imagine having to write a fully-featured single page web application with so much low-level code? This is where *Express* fits in. It is a framework for node.js that will help us write cleaner, more compact code. This is our jQuery on the server side. As soon as our examples become too boringly long, we will switch to Express.

There is another thing we tossed: Apache as an **Application Server**, the part that gave us PHP as a language on the server. We have been generating HTML dynamically on the server using PHP and, by the time the browser read it, it had become all HTML.

The nice part of using PHP was that we could embed PHP code inside plain HTML in between `<?php` and `?>`. Stuffing an HTML file with `<script>` tags to include JavaScript code is not very appealing. We will look at a solution for that as well.

Installing node.js

Let's not delay any further and install node on your computer. How to install it will be different depending on the OS you are running. Go to http://nodejs.org/ and get the proper download. The result is the same everywhere: it gives us two programs: **node** and **npm**.

npm

npm, the **node packaging manager**, is the tool that you use to look for and install modules. Each time you write code that needs a module, you specify this by putting something like the following in your code:

```
var module = require('module');
```

It will have to be installed if it is not yet present, using the command:

npm install

Or you can also use:

npm -g install

The latter will attempt to install the module globally, the former command in the directory where the command is issued. It will typically install the module in a folder called **node_modules**.

node

The node command is the command to use to start your node.js program, for example:

node myprogram.js

Node will start and interpret your code. Type *Ctrl + C* to stop node. Let's get to our first programs right away.

Our inevitable Hello, world example is the smallest possible web server:

```
var http = require('http');
   http.createServer(function (req, res) {
     res.writeHead(200, {'Content-Type': 'text/plain'});
     res.end('Hello World\n');
   }).listen(8080, 'localhost');
   console.log('Server running at http://localhost:8080');
```

Save this file as `hello.js`, or get it from the Packt Publishing website and, in a terminal window, type:

node hello.js

This command will run the program using `node`. In the terminal window, which becomes your console, you will see the text `Server running`.

Next, when you start a browser and type in `http://localhost:8080` as the URL, something that looks like a web page, containing the famous two-word sentence `Hello World`, will appear. As a matter of fact, if you go to `http://localhost:8080/it/does/not/matterwhat`, the same thing will appear. Not very useful maybe, but it is a web server.

Adding HTML

This is a slightly different version where we explicitly specify that we send HTML instead of plain text:

```
var http = require('http');
  http.createServer(function (req, res) {
    res.writeHead(200, {'Content-Type': 'text/html'});
    res.end('<h1>Hello World\</h1>');
  }).listen(8080, 'localhost');
  console.log('Server running at http://localhost:8080');
```

Serving up static content

We are not used to the same thing popping up no matter what path we give as an URL. URLs typically point to a file (or a folder, in which case the server looks for an `index.html` file), `foo.html` or `bar.php`, and, when present, it is served up to the client.

So what if we want to do this with node.js? We need a module. There are several ways to do the job. We use `node-static` in our example. First we need to install it:

npm install node-static

You can typically find documentation on methods and properties on Github and other cool places. In our app, we create not only a web server but a `fileserver` as well. It will serve all the files in the local directory `public`. It is good to have all so called `static content` together in a separate folder. This is basically all the files that will be served up to and interpreted by the client. As we will now end up with a mix of client code and server code, it is good practice to separate them. When you use the Express framework, it will create these things for you.

1. In our project folder we create `hello.js`, our node.js app:

```
var http = require('http');
var static = require('node-static');
var fileServer = new static.Server('./public');
   http.createServer(function (req, res) {
     fileServer.serve(req,res);
   }).listen(8080, 'localhost');
   console.log('Server running at http://localhost:8080');
```

2. Next, in a subfolder `public`, we create `hello.html`:

```
<!DOCTYPE html>
<html>
<head>
<meta charset="UTF-8" />
<title>Hello world document</title>
<link href="./styles/hello.css" rel="stylesheet">
</head>
<body>
<h1>Hello, World</h1>
</body>
</html>
```

3. We can create the background with `hello.css` as follows:

```
body {
  background-color:#FFDEAD;
}
h1
{
  color:teal;
  margin-left:30px;
}
.bigbutton {
  height:40px;
  color: white;
  background-color:teal;
  margin-left:150px;
  margin-top:50px;
  padding:15 15 25 15;
  font-size:18px;
}
```

So if we now visit `http://localhost:8080/hello.html`, we will see our by now too familiar `Hello World` message with some basic styling, proving that our file server also delivered the CSS file.

1. Now we will take it one step further by actually adding JavaScript to our html file (`hellobutton.html` (body only)). We will reuse the previous CSS file, create a slightly different HTML file, and add a JavaScript file. I assume you have a copy of jQuery around somewhere.

```
<body>
<div id="content">
<button type="button" id="hellobutton" class="bigbutton">Click
here for a message</button>
</div>
<script src="js/jquery.js"></script>
<script src="js/hellobutton.js"></script>
</body>
```

2. To add the button, let's create `hellobutton.js`:

```
$(document).ready(function(){
$("#content").on("click", "#hellobutton", function(data){
$('#hellobutton').text("Hello World");
   } );
});
```

So when we go to `http://localhost:8080/hellobutton.html`, we see a web page with a button; when we click on it, its text changes into `Hello World`. This means our client-side jQuery and JavaScript works.

In the `public` folder, create a file `index.html`:

```
<!DOCTYPE html >
<html>
<body>
<h1>It works!</h1>
</body>
</html>
```

If we go to `http://localhost:8080`, we see *It Works !* Just like when we hit the document root of the Apache Web Server. This is because our `node-static` module has that file configured as the default.

But there are other things that do not work the way we are used to. If we type `hellobutton` instead of `hellobutton.html`, nothing will happen, as we did not program our web server to look for `hellobutton.something`. Don't even think of wanting to process `hello.html?key=value`.

On the other hand, if you put a picture file, for example, `baywatchstation.jpg`, in `./public` and type `http://localhost:8080/baywatchstation.jpg`, you will see the picture in your browser. All this is done with very few lines of code and two cool node.js modules.

A tale of two (JavaScript) cities

We have reached an important stage here: we have two different JavaScript files, they are both located on our server, but one is interpreted by node.js and the other one is served up by node.js and interpreted by the browser, in other words the client.

Try this: `http://localhost:8080/js/hellobutton.js`. You will see the code of your JavaScript file in a browser. Now insert `alert("Here's Johnny!");` and put `<script>` tags around it, save it, and refresh your browser. `Johnny` pops up and then JavaScript continues with doing nothing without giving you any error message.

Because we configured `public` (well `node-static` did) as our document root of our mini web server, we cannot even reach `hello.js`, rescuing us from potentially greater confusion. I am confident that by now you understand the difference between a JavaScript file and a JavaScript file. That is why some developers have developed a habit of using different extensions (for example `.njs` for server-side JS files). I believe it is a lot clearer to place the different kinds of files in different folders as we have started doing.

But, so far, in such a short time, and just a few lines of code, we are capable of doing almost anything we discussed in this book up until now, the node.js way: we can handle HTML, CSS, JavaScript, and jQuery. We tossed PHP and we are replacing MySQL with MongoDB. This leaves us just with the latter and Ajax and then we will have, in a way, rewritten our book the node.js way.

node.js and MongoDB

In *Chapter 11*, *MongoDB*, we introduced MongoDB, a document database, and you learned how to access it from the command line as well as from within a PHP program. Doing so in node.js is even easier. First of all, let's not forget to start the MongoDB server inside a separate terminal window:

`mongodb`

Next we need, of course, a node.js module, `mongodb`:

```
npm install mongodb
```

Here follows a simple program that connects to the MongoDB server, the `california` database to be precise, and looks up a document in the `people` collection.

```
var MongoClient = require('mongodb').MongoClient;
    MongoClient.connect('mongodb://localhost:27017/california',
    function(err, db) {
        console.log('Connected to MongoDB!');
        var collection = db.collection('people');
        collection.findOne({name: 'Adams'}, function(err, doc) {
            console.log(doc.first + ' - ' + doc.name);
            db.close();
        });
    });
```

Déjà vu ... once more

As I went through my first steps with node.js, I had a déjà vu experience. To paraphrase the Grace Jones song based on *Libertango* by Astor Piazolla: *Strange, I have seen that happen before.*

With node.js, you only add what you need, so it does not include the kitchen sink by default. This can only mean you will benefit from that as far as performance goes.

I am a UNIX person but this story goes back to when Linus had not yet rewritten it as Linux, Mac OS X did not exist yet, and so on. Memory and disk space were expensive, so was UNIX, as manufacturers had to pay royalties.

I was a proud product manager of a PC UNIX product and one of our coolest value-added things was a tool called **kconfig**, which would allow people to customize what was inside the UNIX kernel, so it would only contain what was needed. This is what node.js reminds me of. And it is written in C, just like UNIX. *Déjà vu.*

Cool as it was then, it would not be cool today, because so much more has been added to UNIX: it would not be manageable.

The same is true if we wanted to mimic everything the Apache web server can handle with pure node.js. Just look at the output of the PHP `phpinfo()` function. It shows all the modules that are loaded into Apache. If we wanted to support all these with with only node.js, we would need too many modules and would end up with unreadable code. The movie Amadeus comes to mind, where the emperor's sidekicks agree on one thing about Mozart's *Le Nozze di Figaro* (I don't): Too many notes!

Express

A good way to get the job done with fewer notes is by using the Express framework. On the expressjs.com website, it is called a *minimal and flexible node.js web application framework, providing a robust set of features for building web applications.*

There probably is no better way to describe what Express can do for you. It is minimal so there is little overhead for the framework itself. It is flexible, so you can add just what you need. As it gives a robust set of features, this means you do not have to create them yourselves and they have been tested by an ever-growing community.

Installing Express

Of course, Express is also a node module, so we install it as such. At the time of writing, we used **Express 4**. In your project directory for your application, type:

```
npm install express
```

Or you can also use:

```
npm install –save express
```

If you specify the –save option, npm will update the package.json file. You will notice that a folder called express will be created inside node_modules and inside that one there is another collection of node-modules. These are examples of what is called **middleware**.

In the few examples that follow, we assume app.js as the name for your node.js application and app for the variable that you will use in that file for your instance of Express. This is for the sake of brevity. It would be better to use a string that matches your project name.

Our first Express app

Of course, we are going to do more Hello, World examples. Here is our first Express app:

```
var express = require('express');
var app = express();
app.set('port', process.env.PORT || 3000);
app.get('/', function (req, res) {
  res.send('<h1>Hello World!</h1>');

});
```

```
app.listen(app.get('port'),  function () {
console.log('Express started on http://localhost:' +
  app.get('port') + '; press Ctrl-C to terminate.' );

});
```

Well, compared to our second node.js example, it is about the same number of lines. But it looks a lot cleaner and it does more for us. You no longer need to explicitly include the HTTP module, you no longer have to specify which header to send, and, when you specify a different URL, you will not get `Hello, World` but a reasonable error message. We use `app.set` and `app.get` for the port. When the environment variable `PORT` is set, the port will be set to its value.

The other line containing `app.get` tells us what we want to happen when the server is presented with a URL in the `GET` mode. Like in node.js, there is a function with the `request` and `respond` objects as an argument. In `express`, they have been extended; there are more creative things you can do with them as there are more methods available to you.

For example, you have access to `req.body`, which will contain an object of all the values that were sent using the `POST` method in a form (using `app.post`).

An example with middleware

We will now use Express to rewrite the `hello button` example. All static resources in the `public` directory can remain untouched. The only change is in the node app itself:

```
var express = require('express');
var path = require('path');
var app = express();

app.set('port', process.env.PORT || 3000);

var options = {
  dotfiles: 'ignore',
  extensions: ['htm', 'html'],
  index: false
};

app.use(express.static(path.join(__dirname, 'public') ,
options    ));

app.listen(app.get('port'),  function () {
```

```
console.log('Hello express started on http://localhost:' +
app.get('port') + '; press Ctrl-C to terminate.' );

});
```

This code uses so-called middleware (`static`) that is included with `express`. There is a lot more available from third parties. In the `req.body` referenced earlier, there is middleware available to parse that form data (`body-parse`). You can also write your own middleware. In its simplest form, it is a function with `req` and `res` as its arguments:

```
app.use (function(req,res) {
    res.status(404);
    res.send(" Oops, you have tried to reach a page that does not
exist");
});
```

This is your minimal 404 handler to give people something meaningful to read on their screen when they type in the wrong URL. You place that in your app.js file after the code that represents the successful scenarios.

Templating and handlebars.js

There is one more `Hello, world` example to go! Throughout the book, we have been using PHP most of the time. We have used it to dynamically generate web pages, or portions thereof. So PHP code, often embedded inside HTML code in a file with `.php` as an extension, is executed on the server and what is rendered by the browser is pure HTML. You also learned how to generate HTML from a separate PHP file or even JavaScript on the client side, using data that comes from the server, and then inject it into a portion of a web page (Ajax).

Combining PHP and HTML and even a small chunk of client-side JavaScript inside a single file was made possible thanks to the `<script>` tag and by putting PHP code in between `<?php` and `?>`. That is why they sometimes call PHP a *templating* language.

Now imagine an all-JavaScript ecosystem. Yes, we could still put our client JavaScript code in between `<script>` tags, but what about the server JavaScript code? There is no such thing as `<?javascript ?>` because this is not how node.js works.

Node.js and Express support several templating languages that allow you to separate layout and content and have the template system do the work to go fetch the content and inject it into the HTML. As we no longer want to learn yet another language, we decided to go with **handlebars.js**, as it uses plain HTML to define your layout, that you already learned some 12 chapters ago. The default templating language for Express appears to be **Jade**, which uses its own, albeit more compact, because there are no tags, format. Another advantage of using handlebars.js is that is also available to do client-side templating.

We conclude this chapter with an example of how you could use handlebars.js.

Our examples in this chapter are all node.js examples, for which we need modules. To use handlebars in node and Express, there are several modules available. I like the one with the easy to remember name **express-handlebars**. If you search the web for handlebars.js, you will find the library to do client-side templating.

Get the `handlebars` module for Express using the following command:

```
npm install express-handlebars
```

Creating a layout

Inside your project folder that contains `public`, create a folder `views`, with a subdirectory `layouts`. Copy other static content you may have from `public` to `views`. Inside the `layouts` subfolder, create a file called `main.handlebars`. This is your default layout. Think of it as a common layout for almost all of your pages:

```html
<!doctype html>
    <html>
    <head>
<title>Handlebars demo</title> </head>
<link href="./styles/hello.css" rel="stylesheet">
<body>
{{{body}}}
    </body>
    </html>
```

Notice the {{{body}}} part. This token will be replaced by HTML. Create, in the views folder, a file called hello.handlebars with the following content. This will be one (of many) example of the HTML, and it will be replaced by:

```
<h1>Hello, World</h1>
```

Our last Hello, World example

Now create a file lasthello.js in the project folder. For convenience, we added the relevant code to the previous Express example. Everything that worked before still works but if you type http://localhost:3000/, you will see a page with the layout from the layout file and {{{body}}} replaced by(you guessed it):

```
var express = require('express');
var path = require('path');
var app = express();
var handlebars = require('express-handlebars') .create({
defaultLayout:'main' });
    app.engine('handlebars', handlebars.engine);
    app.set('view engine', 'handlebars');
app.set('port', process.env.PORT || 3000);

var options = {
  dotfiles: 'ignore',
  etag: false,
  extensions: ['htm', 'html'],
  index: false
};

app.use(express.static(path.join(__dirname, 'public') , options    ));
app.get('/', function(req, res)
{
res.render('hello');    // this is the important part
});
app.listen(app.get('port'),  function () {
  console.log('Hello express started on http://localhost:' +
  app.get('port') + '; press Ctrl-C to terminate.' );

});
```

Summary

In this final chapter, we gave an overview of node.js and Express. Thanks to node.js, you can use JavaScript across the board, on both the client and server side. You can even write your own web server with just a few lines of code. As you only include the things you really need, you can obtain far better performance with this *avant-garde* way of doing web development.

As you combine the web server and the server application in your code, there may be more code to write than you wish for. That is where Express comes to the rescue: a lightweight framework that results in more compact, yet robust code.

To conclude, we touched on the tip of the templating iceberg by introducing handlebars.js. This is a better way to separate layout from dynamic content and have the framework combine the two, so the browser can render it as a view. For that purpose, we concluded the chapter by writing a layout in HTML.

This reminds me of Anna Russell's rendition of Wagner's *Der Ring des Nibelungen*, which she does in 20 minutes (normally the Ring is 16 hours) concluding that the story ends the way it started. It goes a little bit like this:

> There is the Rhine, in the river there are the Rhinemaidens and at the bottom there is ... gold ...

So, after 14 chapters that took us through many aspects of web development we ended where it all started: HTML. I hope you enjoyed reading it as much as I did writing it.

Bootstrap – An Alternative to Foundation

At the time of writing this book, **Bootstrap** was the most popular project on GitHub. Many Web sites and Web applications are built using Bootstrap. Many books have been published on the topic, and often experience in using Bootstrap is required when Web developers apply for a job. That's why I decided to include an Appendix on Bootstrap in this book.

I will walk you through the things that you learned to do with Foundation, but in the Bootstrap way.

Bootstrap components

You can download Bootstrap from `http://getbootstrap.com` in more than one flavor. The smallest download is a simple distribution that contains all the components you need to deploy systems. The source distribution has the same in a subfolder but also contains **docs**, **less**, JavaScript sources, (broken down by component), and examples, all of which make great study material.

Here, we will focus on the minimal distribution. On my system, I have placed them all in the `bootstrap` folder to make it easier to switch releases and to maintain a flavor of Foundation as well as Bootstrap on the site.

 Note that Bootstrap depends on jQuery. Unlike Foundation, the Bootstrap distribution does not come with jQuery, so you need to obtain your copy elsewhere (or use the one that comes with Foundation, of course).

Here's what you will get with the Bootstrap download:

- **css**: This is a folder that contains `bootstrap.css` and `bootstrap.min.css`, Bootstrap's stylesheets. Include one of these in the `<head>` section of your site. In addition, include your own stylesheet. We recommend that you don't modify `bootstrap.css`.

  The folder also contains the stylesheet for the optional *Bootstrap theme*.

- **js/bootstrap.min.js** and **js/bootstrap.js**: This contains all the Bootstrap JavaScript. Put this right before the end of your `<body>` tag.

- **Fonts**: This is a folder containing glyph icons fonts. We stick to the awesome font-awesome fonts.

The Bootstrap grid system

Like Foundation, Bootstrap comes with a grid system that, by default, divides your working screen's real estate into 12 columns. Using classes, you specify how many columns wide you want every block on the screen to be. There are different classes for different sizes; this is Bootstrap's and Foundation's way to make responsive design easy and almost transparent.

Bootstrap and Foundation use different **breakpoints**. With Foundation, small means less than 640 px, medium is from 641 px to 1024 px, and large means 1025 px and higher. There are two optional XL and XXL sizes, like in T-shirts, with breakpoints of 1440 px and 1920 px. The last two are commented out; you need to activate them if you want to use them.

Bootstrap has four sizes: `xs`, `sm`, `md`, and `lg`. Just as two T-shirt manufacturers can have different sizes in small, the two frameworks have different sizes as well, as the breakpoints are 768 px, 992 px, and 1200 px.

 There does not appear to be an equivalent in Bootstrap for a blocked grid.

This is the same example that we showed you in *Chapter 13, Foundation - A Responsive CSS/JavaScript Framework*, but this time it's done in the Bootstrap way:

```
<div class="container">
<div class="row">
<div class="col-xs-12 col-sm-6 col-md-4 col-lg-4">
<h3>First block title</h3>
<p> First block text</p>
```

```
</div>
<div class="col-xs-12 col-sm-6 col-md-4 col-lg-4">
<h3>Second block title</h3>
<p>Second block text</p>
</div>
<div class="col-xs-12 col-sm-6 col-md-4 col-lg-4">
<h3>Third block title</h3>
<p>Third block text</p>
</div>
</div>
</div>
```

Notice that we wrapped the whole row enchilada with a `<div>` with the `container` class. This is how Bootstrap does things. You don't have to add a `column` class, as is the case in Foundation.

Visibility classes

There are a number of visibility classes in Bootstrap, but fewer than in Foundation, to either hide or make parts of your grid visible, as follows:

- `hidden-xs`
- `hidden-sm`
- `hidden-md`
- `hidden-lg`
- `visible-xs`
- `visible-sm`
- `visible-md`
- `visible-lg`

Buttons

In our Foundation examples, we silently used classes associated with **buttons**, defining shape, color, and size. The main class is—surprise, surprise—`button`. Bootstrap has an equivalent set of classes that we will use in the following examples. The main `button` class is `btn`.

Other UI elements

Bootstrap is well-documented; there are many books available as well, to read and learn more. In the remainder of this chapter, we will go over the same UI features that we covered for Foundation, where applicable.

Thumbnails

In Bootstrap, there is a simple class called `thumbnail` that you can use to produce a nicely formatted responsive thumbnail with or without a caption. Take as an example the following code snippet:

```
<a class="thumbnail" href="largeimgs/photo.jpg">
<img src="smallimgs/photo.jpg"></img>
<div><h6>Caption</h6></div>
</a>
```

This puts good styling around your thumbnail image and caption but, once you click on it, the larger image will be shown in a way that is decided by your browser.

Dropdowns

Here's the same drop-down example as before, but the way it is done with Bootstrap. I believe a typo has made it so far into the release that it is now beyond correction. A lover of opera that I am, I cannot find a single aria in Bootstrap; I think they simply meant to say area:

```
<div class="dropdown">
<button  class="btn btn-primary btn-lg" type="button"
id="calpeople" aria-expanded="false" aria-haspopup="true"  data-
toggle="dropdown">California people</button>
    <ul class="dropdown-menu" role="menu" aria-
labelledby="calpeople">
    <li>Ansel Adams</li>
    <li>John Muir</li>
    <li>Arnold Schwarzenegger</li>
    </ul>
    </div>
```

Modal – the Bootstrap popup

Popups can be used anywhere on a site. Bootstrap offers what they call **modals**. It is very similar to the way it is done in Foundation. Here's the Bootstrapped version of the example from before. Notice how the icon to close the popup is handled differently:

```
<div class="row">
<button type="button" class="btn btn-primary btn-md"
data-toggle="modal" data-target="#revealid">
      Click here
 </button>
      <div class="modal fade" id="revealid"  role="dialog" >
      <div class="modal-dialog modal-sm">
      <div class="modal-content">
      <button type="button" class="close" data-dismiss="modal" aria-
label="Close"><span aria-hidden="true">&times;</span></button>
      <p>Text of popup</p>
      </div></div></div></div>
```

Note that the `modal-sm` class is used to determine what we want the size of the modal to be. The `modal-content` part can be divided into three more `<div>` elements: **modal-header**, **modal-body**, and **modal-footer**.

Combining dropdowns and modals

We will now combine dropdowns and modals for what can be part of a photo gallery, as shown here:

```
<div class="row">
<h3> Modal with drop-down for details</h3>
<div class="col-xs-3 col-md-2">
<div class="thumbnail" data-target="#tiogalakepf" data-toggle="modal">
<img src="imagessmall/tiogalakesmall.jpg" alt="Tioga Lake">
    <div class="caption">
    <h6>Tioga Lake</h6>
    </div>
</div></div>
<div id="tiogalakepf"  class="modal"  >
    <div class="modal-dialog modal-md">
    <div class="modal-content">
  <div class="modal-body thumbnail">
    <button type="button" class="close" data-dismiss="modal"
aria-label="Close">
    <span aria-hidden="true">&times;</span></        button>
```

```
      <img  src="imageslarge/tiogalake.jpg">
      <h3 style="text-align:center">Tioga Lake in april of 1997</h3>
       <a class="btn btn-sm btn-primary" data-toggle="dropdown"
   id="tiogadrop" >Details</a>
   <ul class="dropdown-menu" role="menu" aria-labelledby="tiogadrop">
     <li>Hasselblad</li>
      <li> Fuji Velvia</li>
      <li> 40mm CF lens </li>
      <li> f16 </li>
      </ul></div>
   </div></div></div></div>
```

Collapse – an accordion for Bootstrap

Bootstrap's `collapse` feature offers the same functionality as accordion in Foundation and other frameworks. This is how we redid our example. There is little or no styling; so, we suggest that, if you use it with Bootstrap, you combine it with the `panel` widget:

```
<div class="col-xs-12">
<h3>California People</h3>
<a  href="#ansel" data-toggle="collapse">
<h5><i class="fa fa-caret-right green" ></i> Ansel Adams</h5></a>
<div  class="collapse"  id="ansel">
<p>I think of Ansel Adams as the best landscape photographer ever. His
black and white photographs of Yosemite National Park and New Mexico
are legendary </p>
</div>
<a  href="#muir" data-toggle="collapse" >
<h5><i class="fa fa-caret-right green" ></i> John Muir</h5></a>
<div  class="collapse"  id="muir">
<p>I think of John Muir as the father of Yosemite National Park </p>
</div></div>
```

Navigation

Bootstrap has a **navbar** component that you may want to look into. If you like the look of the top shelf bar of Foundation, I encourage you to use the optional *Bootstrap theme*.

Summary

In this Appendix, we described the Bootstrap CSS / JavaScript framework. Like Foundation, it allows you to create a mobile-first, responsive design site or application without having to write any code for the responsive part. We only have to customize the styles to our needs—in a separate style sheet, of course.

Index

readonly attribute 26
value attribute 26
insert_id function 118
installation
node.js 217
Integrated Development
Environment (IDE) 88
Internet Service Providers (ISP) 2
is_dir() function 104
is_file() function 104
iterator_to_array() function 183

J

Jade 226
Java
comparing, with JavaScript 64, 65
JavaScript
about 11, 12, 61
comparing, with Java 64
JavaScript Object Notation. *See* **JSON**
JavaScript program
about 65
control flow 71
expressions 68
functions 74
operators 68
variables 66
jQuery
about 12, 121
and Ajax 132
and event handlers 128
documentation 127
JSON, using with 165-167
library, obtaining 122
location, on page 122
selectors and methods 124-127
URL 122
JQuery Ajax methods
$.ajax() method 138
$.load() method 133
$.post() method 134-138
about 132
jQuery Mobile 122, 123
JSON
about 77, 162, 163
and PHP 164, 165

arrays 164
JSON.parse() method 168
JSON.stringify() method 168
methods 168
number 164
objects 164
strings 164
syntax 163
using, with Ajax 165-167
using, with jQuery 165-167
value syntax 163
values 164

K

kconfig tool 222

L

label attribute 25
LAMP (Linux/Apache/MySQL/
PHP) 109, 215
LANP 215
less
URL 189
library 121
line-height property 49, 50
links, selecting
<a> name attribute 21
<a> target attribute 21
about 20
href attribute, using 20
lists, placing
about 22, 59
list-style-image property 59
list-style-position property 59
list-style-type property 59
load() function 174, 178
loadScripts 198
loadStyles 198

M

margin, box model
about 52-55
collapsing 55-57
properties 54
setting, to auto 54

Thank you for buying
Practical Web Development

About Packt Publishing

Packt, pronounced 'packed', published its first book, *Mastering phpMyAdmin for Effective MySQL Management*, in April 2004, and subsequently continued to specialize in publishing highly focused books on specific technologies and solutions.

Our books and publications share the experiences of your fellow IT professionals in adapting and customizing today's systems, applications, and frameworks. Our solution-based books give you the knowledge and power to customize the software and technologies you're using to get the job done. Packt books are more specific and less general than the IT books you have seen in the past. Our unique business model allows us to bring you more focused information, giving you more of what you need to know, and less of what you don't.

Packt is a modern yet unique publishing company that focuses on producing quality, cutting-edge books for communities of developers, administrators, and newbies alike. For more information, please visit our website at www.packtpub.com.

Writing for Packt

We welcome all inquiries from people who are interested in authoring. Book proposals should be sent to author@packtpub.com. If your book idea is still at an early stage and you would like to discuss it first before writing a formal book proposal, then please contact us; one of our commissioning editors will get in touch with you.

We're not just looking for published authors; if you have strong technical skills but no writing experience, our experienced editors can help you develop a writing career, or simply get some additional reward for your expertise.

Learning Express Web Application Development [Video]

ISBN: 978-1-78398-988-1   Duration: 02:27 hours

Build powerful and modern web apps that run smoothly on the webserver with Express.js

Learning Express Web Application Development

Matthew Nuzum

1. Use Express.js and get the best out of JavaScript to build robust server based web apps.

2. Incorporate MongoDB, the blazingly fast document-based database into your applications.

3. Impress your colleagues with production ready code through test-driven development.

Express Web Application Development

ISBN: 978-1-84969-654-8   Paperback: 236 pages

Learn how to develop web applications with the Express framework from scratch

Express Web Application Development

Learn how to develop web applications with the Express framework from scratch

Hage Yaapa

1. Exploring all aspects of web development using the Express framework.

2. Starts with the essentials.

3. Expert tips and advice covering all Express topics.

Please check **www.PacktPub.com** for information on our titles

Learning Bootstrap

ISBN: 978-1-78216-184-4   Paperback: 204 pages

Unearth the potential of Bootstrap to create responsive web pages using modern techniques

1. Understand the various facets of Bootstrap 3.x such as Base CSS and Components in a pragmatic way.

2. Leverage the power of Bootstrap with a mobile-first approach resulting in responsive web design.

3. Optimize and customize your workflow with LESS and jQuery plug-ins.

Bootstrap Site Blueprints

ISBN: 978-1-78216-452-4   Paperback: 304 pages

Design mobile-first responsive websites with Bootstrap 3

1. Learn the inner workings of Bootstrap 3 and create web applications with ease.

2. Quickly customize your designs working directly with Bootstrap's LESS files.

3. Leverage Bootstrap's excellent JavaScript plugins.

Please check **www.PacktPub.com** for information on our titles

www.ingramcontent.com/pod-product-compliance
Lightning Source LLC
Chambersburg PA
CBHW060529060326
40690CB00017B/3428